C-863   CAREER EXAMINATION SERIES

This is your
PASSBOOK for...

School Purchasing Agent

Test Preparation Study Guide
Questions & Answers

NATIONAL LEARNING CORPORATION®

COPYRIGHT NOTICE

This book is SOLELY intended for, is sold ONLY to, and its use is RESTRICTED to individual, bona fide applicants or candidates who qualify by virtue of having seriously filed applications for appropriate license, certificate, professional and/or promotional advancement, higher school matriculation, scholarship, or other legitimate requirements of education and/or governmental authorities.

This book is NOT intended for use, class instruction, tutoring, training, duplication, copying, reprinting, excerption, or adaptation, etc., by:

1) Other publishers
2) Proprietors and/or Instructors of "Coaching" and/or Preparatory Courses
3) Personnel and/or Training Divisions of commercial, industrial, and governmental organizations
4) Schools, colleges, or universities and/or their departments and staffs, including teachers and other personnel
5) Testing Agencies or Bureaus
6) Study groups which seek by the purchase of a single volume to copy and/or duplicate and/or adapt this material for use by the group as a whole without having purchased individual volumes for each of the members of the group
7) Et al.

Such persons would be in violation of appropriate Federal and State statutes.

PROVISION OF LICENSING AGREEMENTS – Recognized educational, commercial, industrial, and governmental institutions and organizations, and others legitimately engaged in educational pursuits, including training, testing, and measurement activities, may address request for a licensing agreement to the copyright owners, who will determine whether, and under what conditions, including fees and charges, the materials in this book may be used them. In other words, a licensing facility exists for the legitimate use of the material in this book on other than an individual basis. However, it is asseverated and affirmed here that the material in this book CANNOT be used without the receipt of the express permission of such a licensing agreement from the Publishers. Inquiries re licensing should be addressed to the company, attention rights and permissions department.

All rights reserved, including the right of reproduction in whole or in part, in any form or by any means, electronic or mechanical, including photocopying, recording, or by any information storage and retrieval system, without permission in writing from the Publisher.

Copyright © 2024 by
National Learning Corporation

212 Michael Drive, Syosset, NY 11791
(516) 921-8888 • www.passbooks.com
E-mail: info@passbooks.com

PUBLISHED IN THE UNITED STATES OF AMERICA

PASSBOOK® SERIES

THE *PASSBOOK® SERIES* has been created to prepare applicants and candidates for the ultimate academic battlefield – the examination room.

At some time in our lives, each and every one of us may be required to take an examination – for validation, matriculation, admission, qualification, registration, certification, or licensure.

Based on the assumption that every applicant or candidate has met the basic formal educational standards, has taken the required number of courses, and read the necessary texts, the *PASSBOOK® SERIES* furnishes the one special preparation which may assure passing with confidence, instead of failing with insecurity. Examination questions – together with answers – are furnished as the basic vehicle for study so that the mysteries of the examination and its compounding difficulties may be eliminated or diminished by a sure method.

This book is meant to help you pass your examination provided that you qualify and are serious in your objective.

The entire field is reviewed through the huge store of content information which is succinctly presented through a provocative and challenging approach – the question-and-answer method.

A climate of success is established by furnishing the correct answers at the end of each test.

You soon learn to recognize types of questions, forms of questions, and patterns of questioning. You may even begin to anticipate expected outcomes.

You perceive that many questions are repeated or adapted so that you can gain acute insights, which may enable you to score many sure points.

You learn how to confront new questions, or types of questions, and to attack them confidently and work out the correct answers.

You note objectives and emphases, and recognize pitfalls and dangers, so that you may make positive educational adjustments.

Moreover, you are kept fully informed in relation to new concepts, methods, practices, and directions in the field.

You discover that you are actually taking the examination all the time: you are preparing for the examination by "taking" an examination, not by reading extraneous and/or supererogatory textbooks.

In short, this PASSBOOK®, used directedly, should be an important factor in helping you to pass your test.

SCHOOL PURCHASING AGENT

DUTIES:

An employee in this class is responsible for establishing and carrying out a central purchasing procedure for a large school district. Work requires the supervision of a small clerical staff engaged in processing requisitions and bids. The incumbent is personally responsible for the preparation of specifications, the opening of bids and recommending and analyzing the award of bids on the basis of the analysis made. Work is performed under the general direction of the chief business official and the School Board with whom the incumbent confers on matters affecting general purchasing policies and procedures; but the incumbent is expected to exercise a considerable amount of independent judgment and initiative in the performance of his duties. Does related work as required.

SCOPE OF THE EXAMINATION:

The written test will cover knowledge, skills, and/or abilities in such areas as:

1. **Principles and practices of purchasing**: These questions test for candidates' knowledge of the principles guiding governmental purchasing operations and the ability to put them into practice. These questions may deal with but are not necessarily limited to such matters as the analysis of bids, the use of specifications, the award of contracts, the analysis of market factors that can affect the cost of a purchase, and the application of a set of rules to determine how to proceed with a purchase. Some arithmetic computation may be necessary. No specific knowledge of purchasing laws, rules and regulations will be required to answer these questions.
2. **Preparing written material**: These questions test for the ability to present information clearly and accurately, and to organize paragraphs logically and comprehensibly. For some questions, you will be given information in two or three sentences followed by four restatements of the information. You must then choose the best version. For other questions, you will be given paragraphs with their sentences out of order. You must then choose, from four suggestions, the best order for the sentences.
3. **Supervision**: These questions test for knowledge of the principles and practices employed in planning, organizing, and controlling the activities of a work unit toward predetermined objectives. The concepts covered, usually in a situational question format, include such topics as assigning and reviewing work; evaluating performance; maintaining work standards; motivating and developing subordinates; implementing procedural change; increasing efficiency; and dealing with problems of absenteeism, morale, and discipline.
4. **Understanding and interpreting written material**: These questions test for the ability to understand and interpret written material. You will be presented with brief reading passages and will be asked questions about the passages. You should base your answers to the questions only on what is presented in the passages and not on what you may happen to know about the topic.

HOW TO TAKE A TEST

I. YOU MUST PASS AN EXAMINATION

A. *WHAT EVERY CANDIDATE SHOULD KNOW*

Examination applicants often ask us for help in preparing for the written test. What can I study in advance? What kinds of questions will be asked? How will the test be given? How will the papers be graded?

As an applicant for a civil service examination, you may be wondering about some of these things. Our purpose here is to suggest effective methods of advance study and to describe civil service examinations.

Your chances for success on this examination can be increased if you know how to prepare. Those "pre-examination jitters" can be reduced if you know what to expect. You can even experience an adventure in good citizenship if you know why civil service exams are given.

B. *WHY ARE CIVIL SERVICE EXAMINATIONS GIVEN?*

Civil service examinations are important to you in two ways. As a citizen, you want public jobs filled by employees who know how to do their work. As a job seeker, you want a fair chance to compete for that job on an equal footing with other candidates. The best-known means of accomplishing this two-fold goal is the competitive examination.

Exams are widely publicized throughout the nation. They may be administered for jobs in federal, state, city, municipal, town or village governments or agencies.

Any citizen may apply, with some limitations, such as the age or residence of applicants. Your experience and education may be reviewed to see whether you meet the requirements for the particular examination. When these requirements exist, they are reasonable and applied consistently to all applicants. Thus, a competitive examination may cause you some uneasiness now, but it is your privilege and safeguard.

C. *HOW ARE CIVIL SERVICE EXAMS DEVELOPED?*

Examinations are carefully written by trained technicians who are specialists in the field known as "psychological measurement," in consultation with recognized authorities in the field of work that the test will cover. These experts recommend the subject matter areas or skills to be tested; only those knowledges or skills important to your success on the job are included. The most reliable books and source materials available are used as references. Together, the experts and technicians judge the difficulty level of the questions.

Test technicians know how to phrase questions so that the problem is clearly stated. Their ethics do not permit "trick" or "catch" questions. Questions may have been tried out on sample groups, or subjected to statistical analysis, to determine their usefulness.

Written tests are often used in combination with performance tests, ratings of training and experience, and oral interviews. All of these measures combine to form the best-known means of finding the right person for the right job.

II. HOW TO PASS THE WRITTEN TEST

A. NATURE OF THE EXAMINATION

To prepare intelligently for civil service examinations, you should know how they differ from school examinations you have taken. In school you were assigned certain definite pages to read or subjects to cover. The examination questions were quite detailed and usually emphasized memory. Civil service exams, on the other hand, try to discover your present ability to perform the duties of a position, plus your potentiality to learn these duties. In other words, a civil service exam attempts to predict how successful you will be. Questions cover such a broad area that they cannot be as minute and detailed as school exam questions.

In the public service similar kinds of work, or positions, are grouped together in one "class." This process is known as *position-classification*. All the positions in a class are paid according to the salary range for that class. One class title covers all of these positions, and they are all tested by the same examination.

B. FOUR BASIC STEPS

1) Study the announcement

How, then, can you know what subjects to study? Our best answer is: "Learn as much as possible about the class of positions for which you've applied." The exam will test the knowledge, skills and abilities needed to do the work.

Your most valuable source of information about the position you want is the official exam announcement. This announcement lists the training and experience qualifications. Check these standards and apply only if you come reasonably close to meeting them.

The brief description of the position in the examination announcement offers some clues to the subjects which will be tested. Think about the job itself. Review the duties in your mind. Can you perform them, or are there some in which you are rusty? Fill in the blank spots in your preparation.

Many jurisdictions preview the written test in the exam announcement by including a section called "Knowledge and Abilities Required," "Scope of the Examination," or some similar heading. Here you will find out specifically what fields will be tested.

2) Review your own background

Once you learn in general what the position is all about, and what you need to know to do the work, ask yourself which subjects you already know fairly well and which need improvement. You may wonder whether to concentrate on improving your strong areas or on building some background in your fields of weakness. When the announcement has specified "some knowledge" or "considerable knowledge," or has used adjectives like "beginning principles of..." or "advanced ... methods," you can get a clue as to the number and difficulty of questions to be asked in any given field. More questions, and hence broader coverage, would be included for those subjects which are more important in the work. Now weigh your strengths and weaknesses against the job requirements and prepare accordingly.

3) Determine the level of the position

Another way to tell how intensively you should prepare is to understand the level of the job for which you are applying. Is it the entering level? In other words, is this the position in which beginners in a field of work are hired? Or is it an intermediate or advanced level? Sometimes this is indicated by such words as "Junior" or "Senior" in the class title. Other jurisdictions use Roman numerals to designate the level – Clerk I, Clerk II, for example. The word "Supervisor" sometimes appears in the title. If the level is not indicated by the title, check the description of duties. Will you be working under very close supervision, or will you have responsibility for independent decisions in this work?

4) Choose appropriate study materials

Now that you know the subjects to be examined and the relative amount of each subject to be covered, you can choose suitable study materials. For beginning level jobs, or even advanced ones, if you have a pronounced weakness in some aspect of your training, read a modern, standard textbook in that field. Be sure it is up to date and has general coverage. Such books are normally available at your library, and the librarian will be glad to help you locate one. For entry-level positions, questions of appropriate difficulty are chosen – neither highly advanced questions, nor those too simple. Such questions require careful thought but not advanced training.

If the position for which you are applying is technical or advanced, you will read more advanced, specialized material. If you are already familiar with the basic principles of your field, elementary textbooks would waste your time. Concentrate on advanced textbooks and technical periodicals. Think through the concepts and review difficult problems in your field.

These are all general sources. You can get more ideas on your own initiative, following these leads. For example, training manuals and publications of the government agency which employs workers in your field can be useful, particularly for technical and professional positions. A letter or visit to the government department involved may result in more specific study suggestions, and certainly will provide you with a more definite idea of the exact nature of the position you are seeking.

III. KINDS OF TESTS

Tests are used for purposes other than measuring knowledge and ability to perform specified duties. For some positions, it is equally important to test ability to make adjustments to new situations or to profit from training. In others, basic mental abilities not dependent on information are essential. Questions which test these things may not appear as pertinent to the duties of the position as those which test for knowledge and information. Yet they are often highly important parts of a fair examination. For very general questions, it is almost impossible to help you direct your study efforts. What we can do is to point out some of the more common of these general abilities needed in public service positions and describe some typical questions.

1) General information

Broad, general information has been found useful for predicting job success in some kinds of work. This is tested in a variety of ways, from vocabulary lists to questions about current events. Basic background in some field of work, such as sociology or economics, may be sampled in a group of questions. Often these are principles which have become familiar to most persons through exposure rather than through formal training. It is difficult to advise you how to study for these questions; being alert to the world around you is our best suggestion.

2) Verbal ability

An example of an ability needed in many positions is verbal or language ability. Verbal ability is, in brief, the ability to use and understand words. Vocabulary and grammar tests are typical measures of this ability. Reading comprehension or paragraph interpretation questions are common in many kinds of civil service tests. You are given a paragraph of written material and asked to find its central meaning.

3) Numerical ability

Number skills can be tested by the familiar arithmetic problem, by checking paired lists of numbers to see which are alike and which are different, or by interpreting charts and graphs. In the latter test, a graph may be printed in the test booklet which you are asked to use as the basis for answering questions.

4) Observation

A popular test for law-enforcement positions is the observation test. A picture is shown to you for several minutes, then taken away. Questions about the picture test your ability to observe both details and larger elements.

5) Following directions

In many positions in the public service, the employee must be able to carry out written instructions dependably and accurately. You may be given a chart with several columns, each column listing a variety of information. The questions require you to carry out directions involving the information given in the chart.

6) Skills and aptitudes

Performance tests effectively measure some manual skills and aptitudes. When the skill is one in which you are trained, such as typing or shorthand, you can practice. These tests are often very much like those given in business school or high school courses. For many of the other skills and aptitudes, however, no short-time preparation can be made. Skills and abilities natural to you or that you have developed throughout your lifetime are being tested.

Many of the general questions just described provide all the data needed to answer the questions and ask you to use your reasoning ability to find the answers. Your best preparation for these tests, as well as for tests of facts and ideas, is to be at your physical and mental best. You, no doubt, have your own methods of getting into an exam-taking mood and keeping "in shape." The next section lists some ideas on this subject.

IV. KINDS OF QUESTIONS

Only rarely is the "essay" question, which you answer in narrative form, used in civil service tests. Civil service tests are usually of the short-answer type. Full instructions for answering these questions will be given to you at the examination. But in case this is your first experience with short-answer questions and separate answer sheets, here is what you need to know:

1) Multiple-choice Questions

Most popular of the short-answer questions is the "multiple choice" or "best answer" question. It can be used, for example, to test for factual knowledge, ability to solve problems or judgment in meeting situations found at work.

A multiple-choice question is normally one of three types—
- It can begin with an incomplete statement followed by several possible endings. You are to find the one ending which *best* completes the statement, although some of the others may not be entirely wrong.
- It can also be a complete statement in the form of a question which is answered by choosing one of the statements listed.

- It can be in the form of a problem – again you select the best answer.

Here is an example of a multiple-choice question with a discussion which should give you some clues as to the method for choosing the right answer:

When an employee has a complaint about his assignment, the action which will *best* help him overcome his difficulty is to
- A. discuss his difficulty with his coworkers
- B. take the problem to the head of the organization
- C. take the problem to the person who gave him the assignment
- D. say nothing to anyone about his complaint

In answering this question, you should study each of the choices to find which is best. Consider choice "A" – Certainly an employee may discuss his complaint with fellow employees, but no change or improvement can result, and the complaint remains unresolved. Choice "B" is a poor choice since the head of the organization probably does not know what assignment you have been given, and taking your problem to him is known as "going over the head" of the supervisor. The supervisor, or person who made the assignment, is the person who can clarify it or correct any injustice. Choice "C" is, therefore, correct. To say nothing, as in choice "D," is unwise. Supervisors have and interest in knowing the problems employees are facing, and the employee is seeking a solution to his problem.

2) True/False Questions

The "true/false" or "right/wrong" form of question is sometimes used. Here a complete statement is given. Your job is to decide whether the statement is right or wrong.

SAMPLE: A roaming cell-phone call to a nearby city costs less than a non-roaming call to a distant city.

This statement is wrong, or false, since roaming calls are more expensive.

This is not a complete list of all possible question forms, although most of the others are variations of these common types. You will always get complete directions for answering questions. Be sure you understand *how* to mark your answers – ask questions until you do.

V. RECORDING YOUR ANSWERS

Computer terminals are used more and more today for many different kinds of exams.

For an examination with very few applicants, you may be told to record your answers in the test booklet itself. Separate answer sheets are much more common. If this separate answer sheet is to be scored by machine – and this is often the case – it is highly important that you mark your answers correctly in order to get credit.

An electronic scoring machine is often used in civil service offices because of the speed with which papers can be scored. Machine-scored answer sheets must be marked with a pencil, which will be given to you. This pencil has a high graphite content which responds to the electronic scoring machine. As a matter of fact, stray dots may register as answers, so do not let your pencil rest on the answer sheet while you are pondering the correct answer. Also, if your pencil lead breaks or is otherwise defective, ask for another.

Since the answer sheet will be dropped in a slot in the scoring machine, be careful not to bend the corners or get the paper crumpled.

The answer sheet normally has five vertical columns of numbers, with 30 numbers to a column. These numbers correspond to the question numbers in your test booklet. After each number, going across the page are four or five pairs of dotted lines. These short dotted lines have small letters or numbers above them. The first two pairs may also have a "T" or "F" above the letters. This indicates that the first two pairs only are to be used if the questions are of the true-false type. If the questions are multiple choice, disregard the "T" and "F" and pay attention only to the small letters or numbers.

Answer your questions in the manner of the sample that follows:

32. The largest city in the United States is
    A. Washington, D.C.
    B. New York City
    C. Chicago
    D. Detroit
    E. San Francisco

1) Choose the answer you think is best. (New York City is the largest, so "B" is correct.)
2) Find the row of dotted lines numbered the same as the question you are answering. (Find row number 32)
3) Find the pair of dotted lines corresponding to the answer. (Find the pair of lines under the mark "B.")
4) Make a solid black mark between the dotted lines.

VI. BEFORE THE TEST

Common sense will help you find procedures to follow to get ready for an examination. Too many of us, however, overlook these sensible measures. Indeed, nervousness and fatigue have been found to be the most serious reasons why applicants fail to do their best on civil service tests. Here is a list of reminders:

- Begin your preparation early – Don't wait until the last minute to go scurrying around for books and materials or to find out what the position is all about.
- Prepare continuously – An hour a night for a week is better than an all-night cram session. This has been definitely established. What is more, a night a week for a month will return better dividends than crowding your study into a shorter period of time.
- Locate the place of the exam – You have been sent a notice telling you when and where to report for the examination. If the location is in a different town or otherwise unfamiliar to you, it would be well to inquire the best route and learn something about the building.
- Relax the night before the test – Allow your mind to rest. Do not study at all that night. Plan some mild recreation or diversion; then go to bed early and get a good night's sleep.
- Get up early enough to make a leisurely trip to the place for the test – This way unforeseen events, traffic snarls, unfamiliar buildings, etc. will not upset you.
- Dress comfortably – A written test is not a fashion show. You will be known by number and not by name, so wear something comfortable.

- Leave excess paraphernalia at home – Shopping bags and odd bundles will get in your way. You need bring only the items mentioned in the official notice you received; usually everything you need is provided. Do not bring reference books to the exam. They will only confuse those last minutes and be taken away from you when in the test room.
- Arrive somewhat ahead of time – If because of transportation schedules you must get there very early, bring a newspaper or magazine to take your mind off yourself while waiting.
- Locate the examination room – When you have found the proper room, you will be directed to the seat or part of the room where you will sit. Sometimes you are given a sheet of instructions to read while you are waiting. Do not fill out any forms until you are told to do so; just read them and be prepared.
- Relax and prepare to listen to the instructions
- If you have any physical problem that may keep you from doing your best, be sure to tell the test administrator. If you are sick or in poor health, you really cannot do your best on the exam. You can come back and take the test some other time.

VII. AT THE TEST

The day of the test is here and you have the test booklet in your hand. The temptation to get going is very strong. Caution! There is more to success than knowing the right answers. You must know how to identify your papers and understand variations in the type of short-answer question used in this particular examination. Follow these suggestions for maximum results from your efforts:

1) Cooperate with the monitor

The test administrator has a duty to create a situation in which you can be as much at ease as possible. He will give instructions, tell you when to begin, check to see that you are marking your answer sheet correctly, and so on. He is not there to guard you, although he will see that your competitors do not take unfair advantage. He wants to help you do your best.

2) Listen to all instructions

Don't jump the gun! Wait until you understand all directions. In most civil service tests you get more time than you need to answer the questions. So don't be in a hurry. Read each word of instructions until you clearly understand the meaning. Study the examples, listen to all announcements and follow directions. Ask questions if you do not understand what to do.

3) Identify your papers

Civil service exams are usually identified by number only. You will be assigned a number; you must not put your name on your test papers. Be sure to copy your number correctly. Since more than one exam may be given, copy your exact examination title.

4) Plan your time

Unless you are told that a test is a "speed" or "rate of work" test, speed itself is usually not important. Time enough to answer all the questions will be provided, but this does not mean that you have all day. An overall time limit has been set. Divide the total time (in minutes) by the number of questions to determine the approximate time you have for each question.

5) Do not linger over difficult questions

If you come across a difficult question, mark it with a paper clip (useful to have along) and come back to it when you have been through the booklet. One caution if you do this – be sure to skip a number on your answer sheet as well. Check often to be sure that you have not lost your place and that you are marking in the row numbered the same as the question you are answering.

6) Read the questions

Be sure you know what the question asks! Many capable people are unsuccessful because they failed to *read* the questions correctly.

7) Answer all questions

Unless you have been instructed that a penalty will be deducted for incorrect answers, it is better to guess than to omit a question.

8) Speed tests

It is often better NOT to guess on speed tests. It has been found that on timed tests people are tempted to spend the last few seconds before time is called in marking answers at random – without even reading them – in the hope of picking up a few extra points. To discourage this practice, the instructions may warn you that your score will be "corrected" for guessing. That is, a penalty will be applied. The incorrect answers will be deducted from the correct ones, or some other penalty formula will be used.

9) Review your answers

If you finish before time is called, go back to the questions you guessed or omitted to give them further thought. Review other answers if you have time.

10) Return your test materials

If you are ready to leave before others have finished or time is called, take ALL your materials to the monitor and leave quietly. Never take any test material with you. The monitor can discover whose papers are not complete, and taking a test booklet may be grounds for disqualification.

VIII. EXAMINATION TECHNIQUES

1) Read the general instructions carefully. These are usually printed on the first page of the exam booklet. As a rule, these instructions refer to the timing of the examination; the fact that you should not start work until the signal and must stop work at a signal, etc. If there are any *special* instructions, such as a choice of questions to be answered, make sure that you note this instruction carefully.

2) When you are ready to start work on the examination, that is as soon as the signal has been given, read the instructions to each question booklet, underline any key words or phrases, such as *least, best, outline, describe* and the like. In this way you will tend to answer as requested rather than discover on reviewing your paper that you *listed without describing*, that you selected the *worst* choice rather than the *best* choice, etc.

3) If the examination is of the objective or multiple-choice type – that is, each question will also give a series of possible answers: A, B, C or D, and you are called upon to select the best answer and write the letter next to that answer on your answer paper – it is advisable to start answering each question in turn. There may be anywhere from 50 to 100 such questions in the three or four hours allotted and you can see how much time would be taken if you read through all the questions before beginning to answer any. Furthermore, if you come across a question or group of questions which you know would be difficult to answer, it would undoubtedly affect your handling of all the other questions.

4) If the examination is of the essay type and contains but a few questions, it is a moot point as to whether you should read all the questions before starting to answer any one. Of course, if you are given a choice – say five out of seven and the like – then it is essential to read all the questions so you can eliminate the two that are most difficult. If, however, you are asked to answer all the questions, there may be danger in trying to answer the easiest one first because you may find that you will spend too much time on it. The best technique is to answer the first question, then proceed to the second, etc.

5) Time your answers. Before the exam begins, write down the time it started, then add the time allowed for the examination and write down the time it must be completed, then divide the time available somewhat as follows:
    - If 3-1/2 hours are allowed, that would be 210 minutes. If you have 80 objective-type questions, that would be an average of 2-1/2 minutes per question. Allow yourself no more than 2 minutes per question, or a total of 160 minutes, which will permit about 50 minutes to review.
    - If for the time allotment of 210 minutes there are 7 essay questions to answer, that would average about 30 minutes a question. Give yourself only 25 minutes per question so that you have about 35 minutes to review.

6) The most important instruction is to *read each question* and make sure you know what is wanted. The second most important instruction is to *time yourself properly* so that you answer every question. The third most important instruction is to *answer every question*. Guess if you have to but include something for each question. Remember that you will receive no credit for a blank and will probably receive some credit if you write something in answer to an essay question. If you guess a letter – say "B" for a multiple-choice question – you may have guessed right. If you leave a blank as an answer to a multiple-choice question, the examiners may respect your feelings but it will not add a point to your score. Some exams may penalize you for wrong answers, so in such cases *only*, you may not want to guess unless you have some basis for your answer.

7) Suggestions
    a. Objective-type questions
        1. Examine the question booklet for proper sequence of pages and questions
        2. Read all instructions carefully
        3. Skip any question which seems too difficult; return to it after all other questions have been answered
        4. Apportion your time properly; do not spend too much time on any single question or group of questions

5. Note and underline key words – *all, most, fewest, least, best, worst, same, opposite,* etc.
6. Pay particular attention to negatives
7. Note unusual option, e.g., unduly long, short, complex, different or similar in content to the body of the question
8. Observe the use of "hedging" words – *probably, may, most likely,* etc.
9. Make sure that your answer is put next to the same number as the question
10. Do not second-guess unless you have good reason to believe the second answer is definitely more correct
11. Cross out original answer if you decide another answer is more accurate; do not erase until you are ready to hand your paper in
12. Answer all questions; guess unless instructed otherwise
13. Leave time for review

   b. Essay questions
     1. Read each question carefully
     2. Determine exactly what is wanted. Underline key words or phrases.
     3. Decide on outline or paragraph answer
     4. Include many different points and elements unless asked to develop any one or two points or elements
     5. Show impartiality by giving pros and cons unless directed to select one side only
     6. Make and write down any assumptions you find necessary to answer the questions
     7. Watch your English, grammar, punctuation and choice of words
     8. Time your answers; don't crowd material

8) Answering the essay question

Most essay questions can be answered by framing the specific response around several key words or ideas. Here are a few such key words or ideas:

M's: manpower, materials, methods, money, management
P's: purpose, program, policy, plan, procedure, practice, problems, pitfalls, personnel, public relations

   a. Six basic steps in handling problems:
     1. Preliminary plan and background development
     2. Collect information, data and facts
     3. Analyze and interpret information, data and facts
     4. Analyze and develop solutions as well as make recommendations
     5. Prepare report and sell recommendations
     6. Install recommendations and follow up effectiveness

   b. Pitfalls to avoid
     1. *Taking things for granted* – A statement of the situation does not necessarily imply that each of the elements is necessarily true; for example, a complaint may be invalid and biased so that all that can be taken for granted is that a complaint has been registered

2. *Considering only one side of a situation* – Wherever possible, indicate several alternatives and then point out the reasons you selected the best one
3. *Failing to indicate follow up* – Whenever your answer indicates action on your part, make certain that you will take proper follow-up action to see how successful your recommendations, procedures or actions turn out to be
4. *Taking too long in answering any single question* – Remember to time your answers properly

IX. AFTER THE TEST

Scoring procedures differ in detail among civil service jurisdictions although the general principles are the same. Whether the papers are hand-scored or graded by machine we have described, they are nearly always graded by number. That is, the person who marks the paper knows only the number – never the name – of the applicant. Not until all the papers have been graded will they be matched with names. If other tests, such as training and experience or oral interview ratings have been given, scores will be combined. Different parts of the examination usually have different weights. For example, the written test might count 60 percent of the final grade, and a rating of training and experience 40 percent. In many jurisdictions, veterans will have a certain number of points added to their grades.

After the final grade has been determined, the names are placed in grade order and an eligible list is established. There are various methods for resolving ties between those who get the same final grade – probably the most common is to place first the name of the person whose application was received first. Job offers are made from the eligible list in the order the names appear on it. You will be notified of your grade and your rank as soon as all these computations have been made. This will be done as rapidly as possible.

People who are found to meet the requirements in the announcement are called "eligibles." Their names are put on a list of eligible candidates. An eligible's chances of getting a job depend on how high he stands on this list and how fast agencies are filling jobs from the list.

When a job is to be filled from a list of eligibles, the agency asks for the names of people on the list of eligibles for that job. When the civil service commission receives this request, it sends to the agency the names of the three people highest on this list. Or, if the job to be filled has specialized requirements, the office sends the agency the names of the top three persons who meet these requirements from the general list.

The appointing officer makes a choice from among the three people whose names were sent to him. If the selected person accepts the appointment, the names of the others are put back on the list to be considered for future openings.

That is the rule in hiring from all kinds of eligible lists, whether they are for typist, carpenter, chemist, or something else. For every vacancy, the appointing officer has his choice of any one of the top three eligibles on the list. This explains why the person whose name is on top of the list sometimes does not get an appointment when some of the persons lower on the list do. If the appointing officer chooses the second or third eligible, the No. 1 eligible does not get a job at once, but stays on the list until he is appointed or the list is terminated.

X. HOW TO PASS THE INTERVIEW TEST

The examination for which you applied requires an oral interview test. You have already taken the written test and you are now being called for the interview test – the final part of the formal examination.

You may think that it is not possible to prepare for an interview test and that there are no procedures to follow during an interview. Our purpose is to point out some things you can do in advance that will help you and some good rules to follow and pitfalls to avoid while you are being interviewed.

What is an interview supposed to test?

The written examination is designed to test the technical knowledge and competence of the candidate; the oral is designed to evaluate intangible qualities, not readily measured otherwise, and to establish a list showing the relative fitness of each candidate – as measured against his competitors – for the position sought. Scoring is not on the basis of "right" and "wrong," but on a sliding scale of values ranging from "not passable" to "outstanding." As a matter of fact, it is possible to achieve a relatively low score without a single "incorrect" answer because of evident weakness in the qualities being measured.

Occasionally, an examination may consist entirely of an oral test – either an individual or a group oral. In such cases, information is sought concerning the technical knowledges and abilities of the candidate, since there has been no written examination for this purpose. More commonly, however, an oral test is used to supplement a written examination.

Who conducts interviews?

The composition of oral boards varies among different jurisdictions. In nearly all, a representative of the personnel department serves as chairman. One of the members of the board may be a representative of the department in which the candidate would work. In some cases, "outside experts" are used, and, frequently, a businessman or some other representative of the general public is asked to serve. Labor and management or other special groups may be represented. The aim is to secure the services of experts in the appropriate field.

However the board is composed, it is a good idea (and not at all improper or unethical) to ascertain in advance of the interview who the members are and what groups they represent. When you are introduced to them, you will have some idea of their backgrounds and interests, and at least you will not stutter and stammer over their names.

What should be done before the interview?

While knowledge about the board members is useful and takes some of the surprise element out of the interview, there is other preparation which is more substantive. It *is* possible to prepare for an oral interview – in several ways:

1) Keep a copy of your application and review it carefully before the interview

This may be the only document before the oral board, and the starting point of the interview. Know what education and experience you have listed there, and the sequence and dates of all of it. Sometimes the board will ask you to review the highlights of your experience for them; you should not have to hem and haw doing it.

2) Study the class specification and the examination announcement

Usually, the oral board has one or both of these to guide them. The qualities, characteristics or knowledges required by the position sought are stated in these documents. They offer valuable clues as to the nature of the oral interview. For example, if the job involves supervisory responsibilities, the announcement will usually indicate that knowledge of modern supervisory methods and the qualifications of the candidate as a supervisor will be tested. If so, you can expect such questions, frequently in the form of a hypothetical situation which you are expected to solve. NEVER go into an oral without knowledge of the duties and responsibilities of the job you seek.

3) Think through each qualification required

Try to visualize the kind of questions you would ask if you were a board member. How well could you answer them? Try especially to appraise your own knowledge and background in each area, *measured against the job sought*, and identify any areas in which you are weak. Be critical and realistic – do not flatter yourself.

4) Do some general reading in areas in which you feel you may be weak

For example, if the job involves supervision and your past experience has NOT, some general reading in supervisory methods and practices, particularly in the field of human relations, might be useful. Do NOT study agency procedures or detailed manuals. The oral board will be testing your understanding and capacity, not your memory.

5) Get a good night's sleep and watch your general health and mental attitude

You will want a clear head at the interview. Take care of a cold or any other minor ailment, and of course, no hangovers.

What should be done on the day of the interview?

Now comes the day of the interview itself. Give yourself plenty of time to get there. Plan to arrive somewhat ahead of the scheduled time, particularly if your appointment is in the fore part of the day. If a previous candidate fails to appear, the board might be ready for you a bit early. By early afternoon an oral board is almost invariably behind schedule if there are many candidates, and you may have to wait. Take along a book or magazine to read, or your application to review, but leave any extraneous material in the waiting room when you go in for your interview. In any event, relax and compose yourself.

The matter of dress is important. The board is forming impressions about you – from your experience, your manners, your attitude, and your appearance. Give your personal appearance careful attention. Dress your best, but not your flashiest. Choose conservative, appropriate clothing, and be sure it is immaculate. This is a business interview, and your appearance should indicate that you regard it as such. Besides, being well groomed and properly dressed will help boost your confidence.

Sooner or later, someone will call your name and escort you into the interview room. *This is it.* From here on you are on your own. It is too late for any more preparation. But remember, you asked for this opportunity to prove your fitness, and you are here because your request was granted.

What happens when you go in?

The usual sequence of events will be as follows: The clerk (who is often the board stenographer) will introduce you to the chairman of the oral board, who will introduce you to the other members of the board. Acknowledge the introductions before you sit down. Do not be surprised if you find a microphone facing you or a stenotypist sitting by. Oral interviews are usually recorded in the event of an appeal or other review.

Usually the chairman of the board will open the interview by reviewing the highlights of your education and work experience from your application – primarily for the benefit of the other members of the board, as well as to get the material into the record. Do not interrupt or comment unless there is an error or significant misinterpretation; if that is the case, do not hesitate. But do not quibble about insignificant matters. Also, he will usually ask you some question about your education, experience or your present job – partly to get you to start talking and to establish the interviewing "rapport." He may start the actual questioning, or turn it over to one of the other members. Frequently, each member undertakes the questioning on a particular area, one in which he is perhaps most competent, so you can expect each member to participate in the examination. Because time is limited, you may also expect some rather abrupt switches in the direction the questioning takes, so do not be upset by it. Normally, a board member will not pursue a single line of questioning unless he discovers a particular strength or weakness.

After each member has participated, the chairman will usually ask whether any member has any further questions, then will ask you if you have anything you wish to add. Unless you are expecting this question, it may floor you. Worse, it may start you off on an extended, extemporaneous speech. The board is not usually seeking more information. The question is principally to offer you a last opportunity to present further qualifications or to indicate that you have nothing to add. So, if you feel that a significant qualification or characteristic has been overlooked, it is proper to point it out in a sentence or so. Do not compliment the board on the thoroughness of their examination – they have been sketchy, and you know it. If you wish, merely say, "No thank you, I have nothing further to add." This is a point where you can "talk yourself out" of a good impression or fail to present an important bit of information. Remember, *you close the interview yourself.*

The chairman will then say, "That is all, Mr. _____, thank you." Do not be startled; the interview is over, and quicker than you think. Thank him, gather your belongings and take your leave. Save your sigh of relief for the other side of the door.

How to put your best foot forward

Throughout this entire process, you may feel that the board individually and collectively is trying to pierce your defenses, seek out your hidden weaknesses and embarrass and confuse you. Actually, this is not true. They are obliged to make an appraisal of your qualifications for the job you are seeking, and they want to see you in your best light. Remember, they must interview all candidates and a non-cooperative candidate may become a failure in spite of their best efforts to bring out his qualifications. Here are 15 suggestions that will help you:

1) Be natural – Keep your attitude confident, not cocky

If you are not confident that you can do the job, do not expect the board to be. Do not apologize for your weaknesses, try to bring out your strong points. The board is interested in a positive, not negative, presentation. Cockiness will antagonize any board member and make him wonder if you are covering up a weakness by a false show of strength.

2) Get comfortable, but don't lounge or sprawl

Sit erectly but not stiffly. A careless posture may lead the board to conclude that you are careless in other things, or at least that you are not impressed by the importance of the occasion. Either conclusion is natural, even if incorrect. Do not fuss with your clothing, a pencil or an ashtray. Your hands may occasionally be useful to emphasize a point; do not let them become a point of distraction.

3) Do not wisecrack or make small talk

This is a serious situation, and your attitude should show that you consider it as such. Further, the time of the board is limited – they do not want to waste it, and neither should you.

4) Do not exaggerate your experience or abilities

In the first place, from information in the application or other interviews and sources, the board may know more about you than you think. Secondly, you probably will not get away with it. An experienced board is rather adept at spotting such a situation, so do not take the chance.

5) If you know a board member, do not make a point of it, yet do not hide it

Certainly you are not fooling him, and probably not the other members of the board. Do not try to take advantage of your acquaintanceship – it will probably do you little good.

6) Do not dominate the interview

Let the board do that. They will give you the clues – do not assume that you have to do all the talking. Realize that the board has a number of questions to ask you, and do not try to take up all the interview time by showing off your extensive knowledge of the answer to the first one.

7) Be attentive

You only have 20 minutes or so, and you should keep your attention at its sharpest throughout. When a member is addressing a problem or question to you, give him your undivided attention. Address your reply principally to him, but do not exclude the other board members.

8) Do not interrupt

A board member may be stating a problem for you to analyze. He will ask you a question when the time comes. Let him state the problem, and wait for the question.

9) Make sure you understand the question

Do not try to answer until you are sure what the question is. If it is not clear, restate it in your own words or ask the board member to clarify it for you. However, do not haggle about minor elements.

10) Reply promptly but not hastily

A common entry on oral board rating sheets is "candidate responded readily," or "candidate hesitated in replies." Respond as promptly and quickly as you can, but do not jump to a hasty, ill-considered answer.

11) Do not be peremptory in your answers

A brief answer is proper – but do not fire your answer back. That is a losing game from your point of view. The board member can probably ask questions much faster than you can answer them.

12) Do not try to create the answer you think the board member wants

He is interested in what kind of mind you have and how it works – not in playing games. Furthermore, he can usually spot this practice and will actually grade you down on it.

13) Do not switch sides in your reply merely to agree with a board member

Frequently, a member will take a contrary position merely to draw you out and to see if you are willing and able to defend your point of view. Do not start a debate, yet do not surrender a good position. If a position is worth taking, it is worth defending.

14) Do not be afraid to admit an error in judgment if you are shown to be wrong

The board knows that you are forced to reply without any opportunity for careful consideration. Your answer may be demonstrably wrong. If so, admit it and get on with the interview.

15) Do not dwell at length on your present job

The opening question may relate to your present assignment. Answer the question but do not go into an extended discussion. You are being examined for a *new* job, not your present one. As a matter of fact, try to phrase ALL your answers in terms of the job for which you are being examined.

Basis of Rating

Probably you will forget most of these "do's" and "don'ts" when you walk into the oral interview room. Even remembering them all will not ensure you a passing grade. Perhaps you did not have the qualifications in the first place. But remembering them will help you to put your best foot forward, without treading on the toes of the board members.

Rumor and popular opinion to the contrary notwithstanding, an oral board wants you to make the best appearance possible. They know you are under pressure – but they also want to see how you respond to it as a guide to what your reaction would be under the pressures of the job you seek. They will be influenced by the degree of poise you display, the personal traits you show and the manner in which you respond.

ABOUT THIS BOOK

This book contains tests divided into Examination Sections. Go through each test, answering every question in the margin. We have also attached a sample answer sheet at the back of the book that can be removed and used. At the end of each test look at the answer key and check your answers. On the ones you got wrong, look at the right answer choice and learn. Do not fill in the answers first. Do not memorize the questions and answers, but understand the answer and principles involved. On your test, the questions will likely be different from the samples. Questions are changed and new ones added. If you understand these past questions you should have success with any changes that arise. Tests may consist of several types of questions. We have additional books on each subject should more study be advisable or necessary for you. Finally, the more you study, the better prepared you will be. This book is intended to be the last thing you study before you walk into the examination room. Prior study of relevant texts is also recommended. NLC publishes some of these in our Fundamental Series. Knowledge and good sense are important factors in passing your exam. Good luck also helps. So now study this Passbook, absorb the material contained within and take that knowledge into the examination. Then do your best to pass that exam.

EXAMINATION SECTION

EXAMINATION SECTION
TEST 1

DIRECTIONS: Each question or incomplete statement is followed by several suggested answers or completions. Select the one that BEST answers the question or completes the statement. *PRINT THE LETTER OF THE CORRECT ANSWER IN THE SPACE AT THE RIGHT.*

Questions 1-10.

DIRECTIONS: For each question 1 through 10, select the option whose meaning is MOST NEARLY the same as that of the word in capital letters.

1. CARBOY is a

   A. bill of lading
   B. large glass bottle
   C. device for cushioning freight
   D. tool used in unloading freight

2. CONSIGNOR is one who _____ goods.

   A. inspects   B. receives
   C. manufactures   D. ships

3. DEMURRAGE is a

   A. charge made for the detention of freight cars
   B. concealed damage of packed goods
   C. material used to support freight in railroad cars
   D. tax levied by government on import of goods

4. HEDGING is to

   A. decrease production in a rising market
   B. protect against loss due to price rise
   C. secure the use of equipment by lease rather than purchase
   D. take advantage of quantity discounts

5. MANIFEST is a(n)

   A. letter requesting permission to defer payment
   B. list of items kept on hand in a stockroom
   C. invoice of a ship's cargo
   D. order to a warehouse to release merchandise

6. RECIPROCAL

   A. contractual   B. mutual
   C. negotiable   D. unrelated

7. STIPULATE

   A. compensate   B. puncture
   C. specify   D. warrant

8. TORT is a

   A. breach of contract
   B. type of furnace
   C. type of invoice
   D. wrongful act

9. VOUCHER is a

   A. a promissory note
   B. a receipt showing payment
   C. oral agreement
   D. authority for an expenditure

10. WAIVE

    A. certify
    B. legalize
    C. relinquish
    D. transmit

11. The *small order problem* refers MAINLY to the difficulty encountered

    A. by staff units with inadequate budgets which do not provide for emergency purchases
    B. in filling a large number of requisitions for relatively low-priced items which must be purchased
    C. in filling one item orders of bulk supplies or equipment
    D. in storing small quantities of perishable items which are delivered on a daily or weekly basis

12. The BASIC distinction between a purchase requisition and a purchase order is that one

    A. indicates that the prices on the vendor's invoice agree with those on the order while the other authorizes the vendor to furnish the item
    B. indicates that the prices on the vendor's invoice agree with those on the requisition while the other requests that an item be ordered
    C. represents a legal commitment by the vendee while the other requests the buyer to make the purchase
    D. represents a legal commitment by the vendee while the other vouches for the proper completion of the purchase transaction

13. A firm which consistently takes full advantage of *cash discounts* will find that generally

    A. bookkeeping costs more than offset money savings
    B. it enjoys an advantageous credit rating
    C. it gets merchandise of much better quality than contracted for
    D. vendors will prefer to do business with other firms

14. *Lead-time* has been defined as the time required from the day a decision is made to replenish the supply to the day that goods are available for use.
    Which one of the following is NOT generally considered to be a technique for reducing *lead-time*?

    A. Arranging for a blanket order with a supplier
    B. Entering into a requirements contract
    C. Establishing a petty cash account
    D. Utilizing established bidding procedures

3 (#1)

15. Holding lead-time to a minimum is a BASIC factor in   15.____
    A. determining the right time to buy an article at the right price
    B. increasing the number of vendors
    C. keeping inventory on hand to a minimum
    D. securing goods of high quality

16. Assume that an agreement is entered into with a vendor to buy a certain quantity of   16.____
    goods at a certain price. After the agreement has been made, but before the goods have been delivered, there is a general decline in the market price of the goods. Another vendor approaches the buyer and offers to sell him the identical goods at a lower price.
    In this situation, the buyer should

    A. cancel the original order and invite all suppliers to submit bids to supply the goods in question
    B. notify the original vendor to furnish the goods at the lower price and if he refuses to do so, cancel the order
    C. pay the original vendor the higher price for the goods when they are delivered
    D. purchase the goods at the lower price from the second vendor after immediately notifying the original vendor of the proposed action

17. In the following up on orders of merchandise, a buyer uses the following procedure: 17.____
    When a delivery date has not been met, he takes the order and places it in a folder behind the other orders which are also delayed in delivery. In that way, the order that is the most days behind in delivery is at the top of the pile. The buyer telephones suppliers concentrating on the orders which are most delayed.
    A DISADVANTAGE of this procedure is that

    A. delayed orders should not be placed in a folder but should be transcribed on 3x5 cards and kept in a file box on the buyer's desk
    B. priorities are not assigned to the expediting of orders on the basis of user need
    C. telephone calls should not be made unless the vendor has failed to respond to a reminder postcard and then to a letter
    D. the buyer has neglected to number his orders according to delivery date

18. One would be LEAST likely to use a requirements contract when purchasing   18.____
    A. cleaning supplies   B. foodstuffs
    C. heavy machinery   D. raw bulk materials

19. A buyer who wishes to purchase a small quantity of hardware telephones several retail   19.____
    hardware stores in the neighborhood and asks for the price of such items and when they can be delivered. The prices differ to a small extent. The buyer makes his purchase from the store selling the items at the highest price but offering the swiftest delivery.
    The term which BEST describes such buying is _____ buying.

    A. cost and delivery   B. negotiated
    C. open-offer   D. open market

20. The CHIEF difference between formal bidding and informal bidding is that in one case   20.____
    A. invitations to bid are given to or discussed with a selected list of vendors while in the other case the bid proposal is advertised to the general public without any selection of vendors

3

B. bid proposals are incomplete and are subject to reasonable modification by the buyer while in the other case the bid proposal is complete and not subject to modification unless the original bid proposal is withdrawn
C. bids may be made orally in person or by telephone while in the other case bids must be submitted in writing
D. bids must be submitted on or before the date specified in the proposal while in the other case the date by which bids must be submitted is left to the reasonable discretion of the bidder

21. In which one of the following cases is *cost-plus* buying usually LEAST justified? When

   A. a large subway tunnel is to be built
   B. brand-name foodstuffs are to be purchased in large quantities
   C. large repair jobs are involved
   D. research is a large part of the cost of producing the item

22. The one of the following duties which is LEAST desirable to assign to the regular purchasing staff is suggesting

   A. changes in work methods and manpower utilization that will result in lower operating costs
   B. higher quality goods at a higher price if this will result in savings on total costs
   C. material of poorer quality if it can do a satisfactory job at lower cost
   D. to a vendor that he change his product if this will enable the vendor to meet the needs of the purchase at a competitive price

23. If an agreement specifies *f.o.b. destination,* then the _____ assumes the risk of loss due to quality deterioration before the goods arrive at the destination.

   A. buyer is liable for freight charges and
   B. buyer is liable for freight charges but the seller
   C. seller is liable for freight charges and
   D. seller is liable for freight charges but the buyer

24. Which of the following figures is of GREATEST direct interest to the industrial buyer?

   A. Cost of living index
   B. Expenditures for new construction by industry
   C. Industrial production index
   D. Wholesale price index

25. The Gross National Product represents MOST NEARLY the total

   A. cost of goods sold adjusted for changes in the purchasing power of the dollar
   B. industrial production for the nation exclusive of the value of minerals mined
   C. national expenditure for goods and services at current market prices
   D. national income summarizing all earning by labor and property

26. The Consumer Price Index published by the Bureau of Labor Statistics does NOT indicate the

    A. amount of money spent by consumers
    B. average change in the price of goods
    C. changes in the cost of services to the consumer
    D. cost of living

27. Primary responsibility for the administration of the federal anti-trust laws, such as the Sherman and the Clayton Acts, rests with the

    A. Attorney General
    B. Federal Trade Commission
    C. Interstate Commerce Commission
    D. U.S. Department of Commerce

28. The American Standards Association is BEST known for

    A. assisting and coordinating the work of groups interested in developing standards of size
    B. establishing a code of purchasing ethics widely followed in the United States
    C. preparing specifications for a wide range of industrial and agricultural products
    D. publishing a monthly newsletter which advises purchasing agents of manufacturing changes in brand-name products

29. A well-known directory which lists American manufacturers alphabetically is the

    A. APPLETON LIST   B. ARNOLD PRODUCTION GUIDE
    C. SEALY-HALL BLUE BOOK   D. THOMAS REGISTER

30. A work which contained an index of manufacturers and suppliers of instructional material and equipment for schools was

    A. Brill's DIRECTORY OF SCHOOL SUPPLY VENDORS
    B. Morphy's CATALOGUES OF SCHOOL SUPPLIES
    C. Patterson's AMERICAN EDUCATIONAL DIRECTORY
    D. Rittersdorf's SCHOOL PURCHASING MANUAL

Questions 31-40.

DIRECTIONS: Each of Questions 31 through 40 consists of a statement which contains ONE word that is incorrectly used because it is not in keeping with the meaning that the statement is evidently intended to convey. Determine which word is INCORRECTLY used. Then, select from among the words lettered A, B, C, or D the word which, when substituted for the incorrectly used word, would BEST help to convey the meaning of the statement.

31. Deviation from normal inventory standards for current operating schedules plus a limiting factor may be the indicated policy for either of two reasons, to insure availability of materials or to protect costs. Whenever normal availability of a scheduled basis becomes impracticable or uncertain, forward buying is the obvious and necessary means of assuring adequate supply.

    A. preferred   B. safety
    C. supply   D. unworkable

32. As a capital investment, the initial cost of supplies has a direct bearing on ultimate costs since it involves carrying charges, determines the cost chargeable to depreciation, and provides the basis on which profitable operation must be calculated. 32.____

   A. amount
   B. based
   C. equipment
   D. expenditure

33. The success of speculative buying depends on the steepness or decline of a price advance, or the recognition of abnormally low price levels, and on the promptness with which materials can be utilized. 33.____

   A. effectiveness
   B. normally
   C. ordinary
   D. rapidity

34. The taking of competitive bids does not always imply that the order will be awarded to the lowest bidder, although there is a strong presumption that this will be the case, since the invitations to bid will ordinarily be issued only to vendors who are considered to be marginal supply sources in other respects. 34.____

   A. bidders
   B. highest
   C. infer
   D. satisfactory

35. From the purchasing standpoint, it is necessary to inspect received merchandise promptly in order to maintain the purchasing schedule. If the delivery is unacceptable, it will be necessary to replace the merchandise on a shorter inspection cycle than normal. 35.____

   A. expedite
   B. longer
   C. procurement
   D. rejected

36. Stores control has a twofold purpose; from the viewpoint of operations, to assure an adequate supply of funds when needed, in balance with requirements, turning over at a reasonable rate, and without the carrying of excessive quantities; and from the financial viewpoint, to minimize the inventory investment at any given time. 36.____

   A. materials
   B. purchasing
   C. rapid
   D. turnover

37. It should be noted that, while the specification is a precise document to be observed exactly in its details the specification policy should be flexible enough to permit review and revision whenever circumstances may suggest the advisability of such action, so as to avoid *freezing* quality standards, thus barring the way to standardization and progress. 37.____

   A. adjustment
   B. fixing
   C. flexibly
   D. rigid

38. Negotiated contracts rather than awards made on the basis of competitive bidding serve to take the emphasis away from price as the chief factor to be considered in a purchase and serve to give play to the exercise of real research, skill and ingenuity in carrying out the bargaining function. 38.____

   A. agreements
   B. informal
   C. procurement
   D. quality

39. The most common utilization of the discount privilege is by buyers who deduct the cash discount after the stated period has elapsed, apparently regarding this percentage as a concession to which they are automatically entitled as a part of price rather than something which must be earned by observing the period within which payment should be made.

    A. abuse B. before C. cost D. extending

40. Since value is a relative matter, it is altogether possible that good practice will suggest the advisability of moving the standard upward on the scale, and that the final balance of judgment will indicate that the right quality to procure for a purpose will be somewhat above the maximum quality measurements that might be set if the utilitarian basis alone were concerned.

    A. best
    C. minimum
    B. downward
    D. significant

41. A purchaser and a seller have long conversations regarding the terms of a sales contract. Later, the purchaser and the seller enter into a written sales contract. Still later, the seller who had prepared the contract sends a copy of the contract to the purchaser. The purchaser studies the contract and realizes that some of the terms differ from those agreed to in conversation. The purchaser wants the written agreement modified to reflect the terms agreed to in conversation; the seller refuses.
    Under these circumstances, the terms of the contract generally can (not) be modified

    A. if the purchaser can establish that the differences between the oral and written agreements are substantial
    B. if the time elapsed between the signing of the contract and the purchaser's protest is not excessive
    C. even though they differ from the terms agreed to orally
    D. unless the purchaser has a witness to support him

42. Of the following, the one which is NOT an essential element of a sales contract is that it

    A. be entered into by competent parties
    B. be in writing
    C. have a consideration
    D. have the mutual consent of the parties as to its terms

43. A supplier offers in writing to sell certain merchandise at a specified price to a prospective buyer. The next day, before the buyer has had a chance to consider the offer, he receives a telegram from the supplier withdrawing the offer. After receipt of the telegram, the buyer wishes to take advantage of the offer since the price for the merchandise is low.
    The buyer may

    A. *hold* the supplier to the offer because a specific offer once made cannot be withdrawn without the permission of the prospective buyer
    B. *hold* the supplier to the terms of the offer because he was not given a reasonable opportunity to consider the offer before it was withdrawn
    C. *not hold* the supplier to the terms of the offer because an offer once made can be withdrawn at any time before it is accepted
    D. *not hold* the supplier to the terms of the offer because the offer was to sell merchandise and not real estate

44. A buyer notices in a journal an advertisement for typewriters which are priced at $450.00 per machine. The buyer wishes to purchase 10 of these typewriters and mails a personal check for $4500 to the typewriter supplier. A representative of the typewriter supplier returns the check in person and states that the $450.00 machines are sold out but that similar machines priced at $600.00 are available. The buyer insists that he be supplied with the $450.00 machines. The representative refuses.
The buyer is

   A. legally entitled to the $450.00 machines if he can establish that the supplier has them in stock
   B. legally entitled to the $450.00 machines even if the supplier has to go out in the open market to get such machines
   C. not entitled to the $450.00 machines because an advertisement is not a legal offer
   D. not legally entitled to the $450.00 machines since the $4500 check was not a certified check

45. A New York firm purchases 15 tons of rice from a New Orleans dealer. Both parties agree that the goods are to be shipped by rail from New Orleans to New York.
In the course of the rail trip, vandals break into a rail car and damage part of the shipment.
Ordinarily, liability for the damages rests with the

   A. buyer and seller jointly
   B. carrier and seller jointly
   C. carrier only
   D. seller only

46. A cotton bed sheet which has a thread count of less than 112 threads to each square inch is termed

   A. back-filled muslin   B. corded percale
   C. combed percale   D. medium-weight muslin

47. The term *selvage* as used in connection with fabrics refers to

   A. adding weight to a fabric by adding starchy filler
   B. fabric edges woven in such a way as to prevent raveling
   C. fabric shrinkage due to washing
   D. turning in worn fabrics to obtain a lower price in the purchase of new fabrics

48. The one of the following which is NOT generally considered to be a hardwood is

   A. birch   B. hickory   C. pine   D. walnut

49. Of the following instruments, the one GENERALLY used to measure the dimensions of a metal part is a

   A. calorimeter   B. hydrometer
   C. micrometer   D. spring balance

50. Veal is meat from a

   A. calf   B. hog   C. lamb   D. steer

KEY (CORRECT ANSWERS)

1. B	11. B	21. B	31. B	41. C
2. D	12. C	22. A	32. C	42. B
3. A	13. B	23. C	33. D	43. C
4. B	14. D	24. D	34. D	44. C
5. C	15. C	25. C	35. C	45. C
6. B	16. C	26. A	36. A	46. A
7. C	17. B	27. B	37. A	47. B
8. D	18. C	28. A	38. C	48. C
9. B	19. D	29. D	39. A	49. C
10. C	20. A	30. C	40. C	50. A

TEST 2

DIRECTIONS: Each question or incomplete statement is followed by several suggested answers or completions. Select the one that BEST answers the question or completes the statement. *PRINT THE LETTER OF THE CORRECT ANSWER IN THE SPACE AT THE RIGHT.*

1. Benzoate of soda used in the preparation of food is a(n) 1.____
    A. bleaching agent
    B. preservative
    C. thickening agent
    D. emulsifier

2. An inspector who wishes to know the *tare* of a can containing food is concerned with the can's 2.____
    A. bursting strength
    B. dimensions
    C. susceptibility to corrosion
    D. weight

3. A poultry buyer who purchases hens weighing about three pounds each and of an age when they are about ready to start laying eggs has purchased 3.____
    A. broilers
    B. fryers
    C. pullets
    D. roasters

4. The net contents of a No. 10 can of fruit weigh MOST NEARLY _____ lbs. _____ oz. 4.____
    A. 0; 10
    B. 1; 13
    C. 4; 2
    D. 6; 10

5. The one of the following which is NOT a kind of eating apple is the 5.____
    A. Baldwin
    B. Bosc
    C. Jonathan
    D. Northern Spy

6. Which one of the following represents classifications of canned vegetables? 6.____
    A. Class 1, Class 2, Class 3
    B. Fine, Medium-Fine, Extra-Fine
    C. Prime, Choice, Commercial
    D. U.S. Grade A, U.S. Grade B, U.S. Grade C

7. In deciding whether to buy a hard-finish or a soft-finish carbon paper, the buyer should realize that a soft-finish carbon paper makes _____ copies at one writing and has a _____ life. 7.____
    A. fewer; longer
    B. fewer; shorter
    C. more; longer
    D. more; shorter

8. Onionskin paper is USUALLY 8.____
    A. 25% Rag, Substance 9
    B. 50% Rag, Substance 13
    C. 25% Sulphite, Substance 9
    D. 50% Sulphite, Substance 13

9. A No. 10 envelope measures MOST NEARLY 9.____
    A. $3\ 5/8" \times 6\frac{1}{2}"$
    B. $4\ 1/8" \times 9\frac{1}{2}"$
    C. $4\ 3/4" \times 11"$
    D. $8\frac{1}{2}" \times 11\frac{1}{2}"$

2 (#2)

10. Linseed oil is COMMONLY used in paints and varnishes as a   10.____

    A. drying agent   B. pigment
    C. primer   D. thinner

11. The one of the following NOT known primarily as a manufacturer of plumbing fixtures is   11.____

    A. American Radiator and Standard Sanitary Corp.
    B. Crane Co.
    C. E.W. Bliss Co.
    D. Kohler Co.

12. The one of the following which was NOT a supplier of drafting supplies was   12.____

    A. Charles Bruning Co.   B. Cheseboro-Whitman Co.
    C. Dietzgen Inc.   D. Keuffel and Esser Co.

13. A manufacturer of aluminum is   13.____

    A. American Cyanamid Co.
    B. J.P. Stevens and Co.
    C. Reynolds Metals Co.
    D. Youngstown Sheet and Tube Co.

14. A firm known PRIMARILY for the manufacture of paint is   14.____

    A. Charles Pfizer Co.   B. Kimberly-Clark Co.
    C. Nekoosa-Edwards Co.   D. Sherwin-Williams Co.

15. The one of the following BEST known as a manufacturer of duplicating machines is   15.____

    A. Diebold Inc.   B. Gestetner Corp.
    C. Bernard Faber Co.   D. Hellerick and Bradsby Co.

16. The trademark shown at the right represents a firm PRIMARILY engaged in the manufacture of   16.____

    A. generators
    B. glass
    C. paint
    D. paper

17. The trademark shown at the right represents a firm PRIMARILY engaged in the manufacture of   17.____

    A. cameras
    B. cars
    C. chemicals
    D. containers

18. The trademark shown at the right represents a firm PRIMARILY engaged in supplying

    A. electronic computers
    B. office furniture
    C. power equipment
    D. wool products

18.____

19. The trademark shown at the right represents a firm PRIMARILY engaged in the

    A. communications industry
    B. fabrication of aluminim products
    C. manufacture of drug products
    D. transport of freight by air

19.____

20. The trademark shown at the right represents a firm PRIMARILY engaged in the

    A. manufacture of paper products
    B. manufacture of roller bearings
    C. mining of coal
    D. transport of passengers and freight

20.____

21. Assume that out of a shipment of 135 crates of oranges, 11 crates of oranges do not meet acceptable standards. The percentage of crates of oranges which meet acceptable standards is MOST NEARLY

    A. 8.1%   B. 12.3%   C. 87.7%   D. 91.9%

21.____

22. Assume that a shipment of 35 cases of goods, each containing 72 packages, is to be returned to the manufacturer if more than 3% of the packages prove to be defective. The maximum number of defective packages the shipment may contain in order for it NOT to be rejected is

    A. 74
    C. 76
    B. 75
    D. none of the above

22.____

23. Assume that two shipments of goods arrive at a warehouse. The first shipment contains 280 boxes, each measuring 4" x 8" x 10". The second shipment contains 94 cartons, each measuring 1' x 1' x 4'.
    The total number of cubic feet required to store both shipments is MOST NEARLY

    A. 428   B. 466   C. 804   D. 992

23.____

24. Assume that an agency uses 700 reams of bond paper per month and that it must have a three-month supply of bond paper on hand at all times. It takes 2 1/2 months from the time a supply of bond paper is ordered to the time it is delivered.
    What is the minimum reorder point?

    A. 800   B. 1750   C. 3100   D. 3850

24.____

4 (#2)

25. A dietician wishes to order enough butter to serve 2300 school children at lunch time. 15% of the children will take two pats of butter; 10% of the children will take no butter; the remainder will take one pat of butter. Each pat of butter weighs 3/16 of an ounce. Approximately how many pounds of butter should the dietician order? (Allow no butter for wastage.)

    A. 16   B. 29   C. 35   D. 41

25.____

26. By taking advantage of a series discount of 4%, 3%, and 2%, respectively, a buyer paid $7.17 less that list price for an article.
The list price of the article was MOST NEARLY

    A. $78   B. $79   C. $81   D. $82

26.____

27. Assume that you require 77 dozen felt practice golf balls. Which of the following represents the LOWEST bid for these balls?

    A. 41¢ per half-dozen less a 3% discount
    B. 83¢ per dozen less a $7\frac{1}{2}$% discount
    C. 85¢ per dozen less a 10% discount
    D. $65.00 less a series discount of 3%, 2%

27.____

28. Assume that you require 1,944 rulers, packed 12 to the box, 18 boxes to the carton. Which of the following represents the LOWEST bid for these rulers?

    A. 5 1/2¢ per ruler
    B. 6¢ for the first 750 rulers; 5 1/2¢ for the next 750 rulers; 4 1/2¢ for every ruler thereafter
    C. $11.85 per carton
    D. $110 less series discounts of 2%, 1%

28.____

29. Assume that you require 20 cartons of colored raffia, cellophane wrapped in 1 lb. packages, 50 packages to the carton.
Which of the following represents the LOWEST bid for the raffia?

    A. 8¢ per lb.; 15¢ per carton packing charge; 20¢ per carton delivery charge
    B. 9¢ per lb. less a 3% discount
    C. 10¢ per lb. for the first 150 lbs.; 9¢ per lb. for the next 200 lbs.; 8¢ for each lb. thereafter
    D. $88.50 less a 4 1/2 % discount

29.____

30. Assume that you require 50 yards of table felt, 48" wide, and 12 yards of table felt, 72" wide.
Which of the following represents the LOWEST bid for this felt?

    A. $3.20 per yard (48" wide); $4.00 per yard (72" wide)
    B. $3.40 per yard (48" wide); $4.30 per yard (72" wide), series discounts of 5%, 3%
    C. $3.60 per yard (48" wide), $4.10 per yard (72" wide), 8% discount, packing charge $7.50
    D. $230.00 for the order, 9% discount, packing charge $5.00

30.____

31. If the cost of 3 erasers is 50 cents, the cost of 2 1/2 dozen erasers is   31.____

    A. $1.80   B. $3.75   C. $5.00   D. $3.15

32. A circle graph of a budget shows the expenditure of 26.2% for housing, 28.4% for food,   32.____
    12% for clothing, 12.7% for taxes, and the balance for miscellaneous items. The percent
    for miscellaneous items is

    A. 31.5   B. 79.3   C. 20.7   D. 68.5

33. The cost of a broadloom rug measuring 4 feet by 6 feet, at $63.00 per square yard, is   33.____

    A. $168.00   B. $504.00   C. $376.00   D. $210.00

34. The number of tiles each measuring 2 inches by 3 inches needed for a wall 3 feet high   34.____
    and 5 feet long is

    A. 180   B. 30   C. 360   D. 60

35. A merchant purchased a suit for $240.00 and sold it for $320.00.   35.____
    The mark-up on the cost price is

    A. 25%   B. 33 1/3%   C. 75%   D. 15%

Questions 36-40.

DIRECTIONS: Questions 36 through 40 are to be answered SOLELY on the basis of the information contained in tables A-C and in the accompanying notes.

TABLE A

Town of Crestview

FULL SUSPENSION FILES REQUIRED BY CRESTVIEW SCHOOLS

Name of School	Type and Quantity of Files Required*								
	A	AX	B	BX	C	CX	D	DX	YX
Avondale	8	3	9	6	0	8	7	5	3
Bengale	8	0	6	4	12	9	3	5	2
Burnett	2	2	11	10	4	3	3	1	1
Shady Valley #1	14	20	9	7	0	6	5	1	0
Shady Valley #2	9	10	10	3	2	0	2	6	4

* File Code

  A - Two Drawer   CX - Four Drawer with Lock

  AX - Two Drawer with Lock   D - Five Drawer

  B - Three Drawer   DX - Five Drawer with Lock

  BX - Three Drawer with Lock   YX - Jumbo X-ray File

  C - Four Drawer

TABLE B

PRICE LIST FULL SUSPENSION FILES

Type File and Code*	Number Purchased					
	1 or 2	3 or 4	5	6 or 7	8 or 9	Over 9
A - 12	$42.50	$41.25	$39.75	$39.00	$38.50	$38.00
AX - 13	43.50	42.75	42.00	41.25	40.75	39.75
B - 13	46.00	44.50	44.00	43.75	43.50	42.00
BX - 14	46.75	46.25	45.50	44.75	44.00	43.00
C - 24	55.25	54.00	53.00	52.25	51.00	50.00
CX - 25	56.50	55.75	55.25	55.25	54.00	53.00
D - 25	62.00	60.40	58.60	58.00	57.40	56.25
DX - 26	63.00	62.85	61.75	60.80	60.00	59.25
YX - 32	50.00	49.00	48.00	47.00	47.00	45.00

* FIRST digit code identifies the location of the warehouse. (The digit 1 identifies the Boston warehouse; the digit 2 identifies the Nashville warehouse; the digit 3 identifies the Dallas warehouse.) The second digit of the code identifies the weight classification.

TABLE C

SHIPPING CHARGES PER FILE

Warehouse Location	Weight Classification					
	1	2	3	4	5	6
Boston Warehouse	$1.25	$1.55	$2.10	$3.50	$3.80	$4.50
Nashville Warehouse	1.85	2.25	2.95	3.90	4.30	5.00
Dallas Warehouse	2.07	3.50	3.75	4.20	4.20	5.25

NOTES

#1 On sales totalling over $100 but less than $1,000 a special 6% discount is allowed. On sales totalling $1,000 or over but less than $5,000, a special 5% discount is allowed. On sales totalling $100 or less, no special discount is allowed. Special discounts are applied directly to the price of the merchandise only and not to shipping charges except in the case of files shipped to Shady Valley #1 school when special discounts are from list prices plus shipping charges.

#2 Shipping charges pay for the transportation of the files from the warehouse to the Crestview railroad depot. School-owned trucks pick up files from the railroad depot except in the case of the Burnett school. The Burnett school does not have a truck available and hires a private trucker who charges $2.00 per file for pickup from the railroad depot; no discounts are applicable to this $2.00 charge.

#3 The manufacturer allows special discounts from the bill for prompt payment. If the bill is paid within 10 days, a 3% discount from the bill is allowed; if the bill is paid from 10 to 30 days from billing date, a 2% discount is allowed. The Avondale school and the Shady Valley #1 school do not take advantage of discounts for prompt payment. All other schools pay within 10 days except for the Bengale school, which pays its bills 2-3 weeks after the billing date.

#4 Unless specified to the contrary, all files are olive drab in color. The manufacturer will furnish files painted black for an additional charge of 50¢ per file for two or three drawer files and 75¢ per file for four or five drawer files. Jumbo x-ray files are available in a white enamel finish at an additional charge of $1.75 per file. Color charges are to be added directly to the list price before calculating the special discount.

36. The total price that the Bengale school will have to pay for its required four-drawer files without locks is MOST NEARLY

    A. $564.00   B. $598.59   C. $610.80   D. $623.01

37. Approximately how much would it cost the Shady Valley #2 school to purchase 9 two-drawer files with locks?

    A. $344.75   B. $352.73   C. $363.64   D. $366.75

38. Assume that Shady Valley #1 school decides to order one each of every type of file it requires before placing an order for the balance of its requirements.
    What would this school have to pay for these files?

    A. $360.11   B. $360.48   C. $381.87   D. $383.10

39. Required jumbo x-ray files with a white enamel finish will cost Avondale MOST NEARLY

    A. $143.11   B. $152.25   C. $153.61   D. $162.75

40. How much will it cost the Shady Valley #1 school to purchase all two-drawer files it requires, both with and without locks, if half of the two-drawer files with locks are to be furnished in a black finish?

    A. $1311.96   B. $1322.00   C. $1325.91   D. $1332.00

Questions 41-43.

DIRECTIONS: Questions 41 through 43 are to be answered on the basis of the information contained in the passage given below.

The receiving department should inspect the exterior condition of the packaging when a shipment is received before signing the dray ticket. When it is obvious that the package has been broken or dropped and there is apparent damage, this fact should be noted on such dray ticket. A clear receipt should not be given the carrier's representative unless the package, to all outward appearances, is undamaged. If the package is received in an undamaged condition and at a later date it is discovered that the material within the package is damaged, such concealed damage still gives the receiver an opportunity to make claim against the transportation company. However, a claim of concealed damage is more difficult to substantiate. When concealed damage is discovered, the carrier should be notified promptly of this fact by telephone and a claim as well as a request for inspection should be made. Carriers usually insist that all packaging materials and cartons be retained by the receiving department until this inspection has been made by the carrier. Should the carrier decline the opportunity to inspect the damaged shipment, he merely informs the receiving department to go ahead and proceed with filing a claim. A claim number should be obtained when making such a telephone call.

41. Of the following, the MOST suitable title for the foregoing passage is 41.____

    A. Acceptance of Material Upon Receipt
    B. Essentials of Proper Packaging
    C. Procedure for Returning Damaged Merchandise
    D. The Importance of the Dray Ticket in Securing Compensation for Damages

42. Of the following, the BEST evidence that the carrier had been notified of the existence of concealed damage would probably be the 42.____

    A. claim number
    B. defective merchandise
    C. dray ticket
    D. packaging materials if defective

43. Of the following, the MOST likely reason for the carrier's insistence that packaging materials be retained in the event of concealed damage until the carrier has made the inspection is that the carrier may 43.____

    A. be able to advise the supplier of the need to be more careful in the future in the selection of packaging materials
    B. be better able to train his employees in more efficient materials handling techniques
    C. have evidence in the event of an action by the carrier against the supplier
    D. utilize the same packaging materials in returning the defective merchandise to the supplier

Questions 44-46.

DIRECTIONS: Questions 44 through 46 are to be answered on the basis of the information contained in the passage given below.

The use of a recognized brand name to describe a need is a method familiar to school purchasing officials. This is a simple though not always satisfactory ordering description. It has the advantage of being more readily understood by the supplier, and the buyer can be assured of obtaining the desired manufacturer's product. The difficulty of attempting to express specific physical or chemical requirements is eliminated by accepting the manufacturer's formula. User acceptance may be more readily obtained because an established and familiar product is procured. A disadvantage of this method is that it eliminates competition at the manufacturer's level.

A purchasing agent often has the feeling that unless he makes complete use of purchase specifications he is not doing an adequate buying job. Nothing is further from the truth. The other methods of describing quality are often used by the practicing purchasing agent. Not all requirements can be reduced to specific terms. Small purchases, of which schools have many, are not economically acquired by the use of purchase specifications because of the cost of preparing such specifications. It must also be remembered that when the purchaser does buy by specifications, he assumes responsibility for the performance of the product he specifies, since he has drawn the rules of how it is to be made and what its composition will be. Wise selection of the method of describing quality is perhaps a more essential prerequisite for a purchasing agent than the ability to prepare purchase specifications for each item he buys.

44. Of the following, the MOST suitable title for the foregoing passage would be 44.____

    A. Advantages of Buying By Specification
    B. Buying in Small Quantities
    C. Methods of Purchasing
    D. Preparing the Purchase Specification

45. An advantage of buying by the use of a purchase specification implied by the author is that 45.____

    A. brand-name merchandise is more likely to carry a warranty
    B. certain purchasing requirements cannot be expressed in writing with a high degree of precision
    C. it often enables purchasing in quantity at a lower cost based on specific needs
    D. purchase specifications can readily be prepared

46. According to the foregoing passage, an advantage of purchasing by brand name implied by the author is that 46.____

    A. brand-name merchandise is nearly always more suited for long-term usage than unbranded merchandise
    B. it encourages bidding by manufacturers of like products
    C. manufacturers of brand-name preparations change the formulas of their products
    D. persons generally prefer using a well-known item

Questions 47-50.

DIRECTIONS: Questions 47 through 50 are to be answered on the basis of the information contained in the passage given below.

In the late fifties, the average American housewife spent $4.50 per day for a family of four on food and 5.15 hours in food preparation, if all of her food was *home prepared;* she spent $5.80 per day and 3.25 hours if all of her food was purchased *partially prepared,* and $6.70 per day and 1.65 hours if all of her food was purchased *ready-to-serve.*

Americans spent about 20 billion dollars for food products in 1941. They spent nearly 70 billion dollars in 1958. They spent 25 percent of their cash income on food in 1958. For the same kinds and quantities of food that consumers bought in 1941, they would have spent only 16% of their cash income in 1958. It is obvious that our food does cost more. Many factors contribute to this increase besides the additional cost that might be attributed to processing. Consumption of more expensive food items, higher marketing margins, and more food eaten in restaurants are other factors.

The Census of Manufacturers gives some indication of the total bill for processing. The value added by manufacturing of food and kindred products amounted to 3.5 billion of the 20 billion dollars spent for food in 1941. In the year 1958, the comparable figure had climbed to 14 billion dollars.

47. According to the foregoing passage, the cash income of Americans in 1958 was MOST NEARLY _____ billion dollars.

   A. 11.2   B. 17.5   C. 70   D. 280

48. According to the foregoing passage, if Americans bought the same kinds and quantities of food in 1958 as they did in 1941, they would have spent MOST NEARLY _____ billion dollars.

   A. 20   B. 45   C. 74   D. 84

49. According to the foregoing passage, the percent increase in money spent for food in 1958 over 1941 as compared with the percentage increase in money spent for food processing in the same years

   A. was greater
   B. was less
   C. was the same
   D. cannot be determined from the passage

50. In 1958 an American housewife who bought all of her food ready-to-serve saved in time, as compared with the housewife who prepared all of her food at home,

   A. 1.6 hours daily
   B. 1.9 hours daily
   C. 3.5 hours daily
   D. an amount of time which cannot be determined from the foregoing passage

KEY (CORRECT ANSWERS)

1. B	11. C	21. D	31. C	41. A
2. D	12. B	22. B	32. C	42. A
3. C	13. C	23. A	33. A	43. C
4. D	14. D	24. D	34. C	44. C
5. B	15. B	25. B	35. B	45. C
6. D	16. B	26. D	36. B	46. D
7. D	17. D	27. C	37. B	47. D
8. A	18. B	28. B	38. A	48. B
9. B	19. C	29. D	39. C	49. B
10. A	20. A	30. B	40. A	50. C

EXAMINATION SECTION
TEST 1

DIRECTIONS: Each question or incomplete statement is followed by several suggested answers or completions. Select the one that BEST answers the question or completes the statement. *PRINT THE LETTER OF THE CORRECT ANSWER IN THE SPACE AT THE RIGHT.*

1. Which one of the following is NOT an advantage of centralized purchasing?   1.____

    A. Preferential discounts can be secured for quantity contracts.
    B. Higher yields are obtained from disposal of excess surplus, scrap, and salvage.
    C. Savings from elimination of duplicated personnel are effected.
    D. Purchases are made more directly and promptly.

2. Of the following, the record that has the LEAST relevancy to the purchasing procedure is the   2.____

    A. commodity purchase record
    B. purchase requisition
    C. request for quotation
    D. stores requisition

3. While quantity purchases generally represent a saving over smaller purchases, an astute buyer realizes that many facts must be considered before seeking price reduction through quantity alone.   3.____
Of the chief factors to be considered, the one which is of LEAST importance is

    A. obsolescence   B. handling and distribution
    C. price analysis   D. possible deterioration

4. The one of the following factors which should be LEAST considered when selecting a bid is   4.____

    A. responsibility of the bidder
    B. price, discounts, and quality of material offered
    C. capacity of the bidder to engage in reciprocity
    D. delivery date

5. If you are considering the names *IBM* and *Smith-Corona* as possible sources of supply for a certain item, the one of the following which you would MOST probably add to the list is   5.____

    A. Admiral   B. 3M   C. Toshiba   D. Olivetti

6. Which one of the following is it LEAST important to consider when selecting the right vendor?   6.____

    A. Maintenance costs of a higher bidder are significantly lower than that of the lowest bidder.
    B. The vendor has a tax hearing pending with the Federal government.
    C. The vendor has frequent strikes in his plant.
    D. The vendor is often late in making deliveries.

7. After a vendor deposits his bid with the purchasing department, when if at all, may it be withdrawn by him?

   A. At any time
   B. Before the award is made
   C. It may not be withdrawn
   D. Prior to the opening

8. The one of the following which is NOT a publication of value to buyers and purchasing agents is

   A. DUN'S REVIEW
   B. FORBES
   C. FORTUNE
   D. MILL AND FACTORY

9. Which one of the following is NOT a credit reporting agency?

   A. Allen Reports, Inc.
   B. Dun and Bradstreet
   C. Harcourt-Brace
   D. Skip-Tracers, Inc.

10. Of the following, the reference item which is NOT of value in assisting the buyer to determine whether a price bid is fair and reasonable is

    A. commodity journals
    B. price experience
    C. price indices
    D. Sweet's catalogs

11. The term *sellers' market* refers to a condition where

    A. costs of procurement are high but costs of expediting will be insubstantial
    B. economic waste is discouraged
    C. supply is less than demand
    D. there is an overabundance of the materials involved

12. Use of the expression in sales agreement that goods are sold *as is* implies that

    A. buyer will have recourse on the vendor for the quality of the goods but not for the condition
    B. buyer is taking delivery of goods in some way defective
    C. goods offered may be damaged but must be in substantially workable condition
    D. the usual warranty will apply to the transaction if the vendor is guilty of concealment

13. A contract in which buyer and seller both understand that the goods which are exhibited constitute the standard with which the goods not exhibited correspond, and to which deliveries should conform, is known as a sale

    A. by sample
    B. with right of redemption
    C. by consignment
    D. of fungibles

14. The one of the following that is NOT a specification and code-making organization is American _____ Association.

    A. Gas
    B. Management
    C. Standards
    D. Water Works

15. Assume that bids are received for certain castings. The specification on which the bids are based states that a tolerance of 1/32 inch on a certain dimension will be permitted. The buyer knows that actually the castings will be accepted if they are within 1/16 of an inch of the tolerance limit. A prospective bidder on these castings contacts the buyer and asks whether the 1/32 inch tolerance must be adhered to. The buyer informs him that in all probability the castings will be accepted if they are within 1/16 of an inch of the tolerance limit. Such action by the buyer is generally

    A. *ethical* provided he refuses any gifts or favors from the bidder
    B. *ethical* provided the buyer is certain he knows the permitted tolerance limit exactly
    C. *unethical* since the bidder is at a competitive advantage
    D. *unethical* since the buyer has placed himself under an obligation to the bidder

16. *Contract date* is the date

    A. the contract is prepared or typed
    B. the contract is acknowledged by the seller
    C. the buyer returns the contract to the seller
    D. when the contract is accepted by all parties thereto

17. When a buyer wittingly solicits a favored price, discriminatory to other competing customers, he may be in violation of the

    A. Clayton Act, as amended
    B. Food, Drug, and Cosmetic Act
    C. Federal Trade Commission Act
    D. Sherman Anti-Trust Act

18. Of the following elements, which is LEAST necessary in order for a contract to be valid and binding?

    A. Competent parties
    B. Consideration
    C. Legality of subject matter
    D. Written acceptance

19. A *standard package discount* refers to the discount allowed

    A. according to the number of packages purchased
    B. if the purchaser agreed to buy the vendor's regular package
    C. on the package content determined by the buyer
    D. when more than one of an item is purchased

20. Which one of the following defines the term *cost-plus* best?
    The

    A. cost to produce the item plus a stated percentage of fixed sum
    B. cost to produce the item plus packing costs
    C. cost to produce the item plus shipping costs
    D. original cost of the item to the buyer plus all costs involved until it is ultimately used

21. When an item is shipped on *consignment*,

    A. the item becomes part of the buyer's inventory
    B. the purchaser must pay for the item upon receipt
    C. title in the item remains with the seller
    D. title passes to the buyer upon receipt of the item

22. The term *escalation* means which one of the following? A provision   22.____

    A. allowing for an increase in a contract price based on pre-determined contingencies
    B. for increasing the rate of payments due under a purchase contract
    C. for increasing the rate of production on a purchase requirement resulting in earlier deliveries
    D. for requiring earlier than contracted for deliveries

23. Of the following, the term *liquidated damages* is BEST defined as   23.____

    A. a sum agreed upon between the buyer and seller to be paid by the party who breaches the contract
    B. a varying amount which is to be paid by the seller to the buyer if the commodity is seized or destroyed by governmental authority
    C. the costs assessed when a liquid commodity is damaged during return shipment to the manufacturer
    D. the costs assessed when a liquid commodity is damaged prior to receipt by the purchaser

24. When used in the field of transportation, the term *prepaid* means MOST NEARLY the   24.____

    A. purchaser agrees to pay all costs involved in the purchase, including the cost of the service or item plus transportation costs, prior to shipment being made
    B. purchaser has agreed to pay all transportation charges involved in the purchase prior to receipt of the goods
    C. seller has agreed to pay all return transportation charges if the buyer later decides not to accept the goods
    D. seller has agreed to pay all transportation charges involved in the purchase

25. Which of the following statements is FALSE?   25.____

    A. Brass is an alloy of copper and zinc.
    B. Bronze is an alloy of copper and tin.
    C. Mild steel is also known as low carbon steel.
    D. Stainless steel pipe type 304 weighs about the same as steel pipe given the same thickness and length.

26. With respect to purchases of glass, *Type I* refers to   26.____

    A. price
    B. resistance to breakage
    C. resistance to high temperatures and chemicals
    D. size

27. Paper is *calendared* to   27.____

    A. impress the logotype of the mill on it
    B. make it smooth
    C. permit successive pages to be consecutively numbered
    D. record the date of its manufacture

28. The term *prime contractor* refers to the

    A. firm with which the city has entered into a direct contract for supplies and materials
    B. firm that undertakes to perform a job but which releases control of the means and manner of accomplishing the desired result
    C. first vendor to submit a price
    D. vendor who manufactures against a sub-contract

29. A manufacturer's agent

    A. cannot spread costs over a number of lines
    B. represents the purchaser
    C. serves as a manufacturer's sales organization
    D. takes title to merchandise he sells

30. The abbreviation LCL is MOST closely associated with which one of the following modes of transportation?

    A. Air   B. Rail   C. Ship   D. Truck

31. The term *2 percent E.O.M. - 10* means that

    A. if an error or omission is reported by the buyer within 10 days of receipt of a shipment, a 2 percent discount is allowed
    B. a 2 percent discount is allowed if payment is made on or before the 10th of the following month
    C. a 2 percent discount is allowed if payment is made on or before the 10th day of the month in which shipment is made whether or not the shipment has been received
    D. a 2 percent discount is allowed if the invoice is paid within 10 days of its receipt

32. In a *conditional* sale,

    A. possession only of the item is retained by the seller
    B. the title and possession is retained by the seller
    C. the title and possession passes to the purchaser
    D. the title only is retained by the seller

33. Which one of the following is NOT a method of specification? Specification by

    A. chemical analysis   B. custom
    C. physical description   D. sample

Questions 34-36.

DIRECTIONS: Questions 34 through 36 are to be answered on the basis of the following passage.

The State Assembly has passed a bill that would require all state agencies, public authoritites, and local governments to refuse bids in excess of $2,000 from any foreign firm or corporation. The only exceptions to this outright prohibition against public buying of foreign goods or services would be for products not available in this country, goods of a quality unobtainable from an American supplier, and products using foreign materials that are *substantially* manufactured in the United States.

The bill is a flagrant violation of the United States' officially espoused trade principles. It would add to the costs of state and local governments. It could provoke retaliatory action from many foreign governments against the state and other American producers, and foreign governments would be fully entitled to take such retaliatory action under the General Agreement on Tariffs and Trade, which the United States has signed.

The State Senate, which now has the Assembly bill before it, should reject this protectionist legislation out of enlightened regard for the interests of the taxpayers and producers of the state—as well as for those of the nation and its trading partners generally. In this time of unemployment and international monetary disorder, the state—with its reputation for intelligent and progressive law-making—should avoid contributing to what could become a tidal wave of protectionism here and overseas.

34. Under the requirements of the bill passed by the State Assembly, a bid from a foreign manufacturer in excess of $2,000 can be accepted by a state agency or local government only if it meets which one of the following requirements?
The

   A. bid is approved individually by the state legislature
   B. bidder is willing to accept payment in United States currency
   C. bid is for an item of a quality unobtainable from an American supplier
   D. bid is for an item which would be more expensive if it were purchased from an American supplier

35. The author of the above passage feels that the bill passed by the State Assembly should be

   A. passed by the State Senate and put into effect
   B. passed by the State Senate but vetoed by the Governor
   C. reintroduced into the State Assembly and rejected
   D. rejected by the State Senate

36. The author of the passage calls the practice of prohibiting purchase of products manufactured by foreign countries

   A. prohibition
   C. retaliatory action
   B. protectionism
   D. isolationism

37. Of the following, the one that defines *buyer's option* best is:
The

   A. buyer may purchase the item or items at his convenience
   B. buyer must effectuate the purchase sooner or later
   C. price, time, and conditions are usually agreed upon in advance
   D. price to be paid will be determined at the time the option is exercised

38. Proprietary article is a(n)

   A. article manufactured and sold by a patentee
   B. franchised item
   C. individual piece or thing of a class
   D. medicinal compound

39. Assume that it is necessary to partition a room measuring 40 feet by 20 feet into eight smaller rooms of equal size. Allowing no room for aisles, the MINIMUM amount of partitioning that would be needed is _____ feet.

   A. 90   B. 100   C. 110   D. 140

40. Assume that two types of files have been ordered: 200 of type A and 100 of type B. When the files are delivered, the buyer discovers that 25% of each type is damaged. Of the remaining files, 20% of type A and 40% of type B are the wrong color. The total number of files that are the WRONG color is

   A. 30   B. 40   C. 50   D. 60

Questions 41-50.

DIRECTIONS: Questions 41 through 50 are to be answered solely on the basis of the following table showing the amounts purchased by various purchasing units during 2007.

DOLLAR VOLUME PURCHASED BY EACH PURCHASING UNIT DURING EACH QUARTER OF 2007
(FIGURES SHOWN REPRESENT THOUSANDS OF DOLLARS)

Purchasing Unit	First Quarter	Second Quarter	Third Quarter	Fourth Quarter
A	578	924	698	312
B	1,426	1,972	1,586	1,704
C	366	494	430	716
D	1,238	1,708	1,884	1,546
E	730	742	818	774
F	948	1,118	1,256	788

41. The total dollar volume purchased by all of the purchasing units during 2007 approximated MOST NEARLY

   A. $2,000,000   B. $4,000,000
   C. $20,000,000   D. $40,000,000

42. During which quarter was the GREATEST total dollar amount of purchases made?

   A. First   B. Second   C. Third   D. Fourth

43. Assume that the dollar volume purchased by Unit F during 2007 exceeded the dollar volume purchased by Unit F during 2006 by 50%. Then, the dollar volume purchased by Unit F during 2006 was

   A. $2,055,000   B. $2,550,000
   C. $2,740,000   D. $6,165,000

44. Which one of the following purchasing units showed the sharpest DECREASE in the amount purchased during the fourth quarter as compared with the third quarter? Unit

   A. A   B. B   C. D   D. E

45. Comparing the dollar volume purchased in the second quarter with the dollar volume purchased in the third quarter, the decrease in the dollar volume during the third quarter was PRIMARILY due to the decrease in the dollar volume purchased by Units _____ and _____.

   A. A; B   B. C; D   C. C; E   D. C; F

46. Of the following, the unit which had the LARGEST number of dollars of increased purchases from any one quarter to the next following quarter was Unit

   A. A   B. B   C. C   D. D

47. Of the following, the unit with the LARGEST dollar volume of purchases during the second half of 2007 was Unit

   A. A   B. B   C. D   D. F

48. Which one of the following MOST closely approximates the percentage which Unit B's total 2007 purchases represents of the total 2007 purchases of all units, including Unit B?

   A. 10%   B. 15%   C. 25%   D. 45%

49. Assume that research showed that each ten thousand dollars ($10,000) of purchases by Unit D during 2007 required an average of thirteen (13) man-hours of buyers' staff time. On that basis, which one of the following MOST closely approximates the number of man-hours of buyers' staff time required by Unit D during 2007? _____ man-hours.

   A. 1,800   B. 8,000   C. 68,000   D. 78,000

50. Assume that research showed that each ten thousand dollars ($10,000) of purchases by Unit C during 2007 required an average of ten (10) man-hours of buyers' staff time. This research also showed that during 2007 the average man-hours of buyers' staff time per ten thousand dollars of purchases required by Unit C exceeded by 25% the average man-hours of buyers' staff time per ten thousand dollars of purchases required by Unit E. On that basis, which one of the following MOST closely approximates the number of buyers' staff man-hours required by Unit E during 2007? _____ man-hours.

   A. 2,200   B. 2,400   C. 3,000   D. 3,700

KEY (CORRECT ANSWERS)

1. D	11. C	21. C	31. B	41. C
2. D	12. B	22. A	32. D	42. B
3. C	13. A	23. A	33. B	43. C
4. C	14. B	24. D	34. C	44. A
5. D	15. C	25. C	35. D	45. A
6. A	16. D	26. C	36. B	46. B
7. D	17. A	27. B	37. C	47. C
8. B	18. D	28. A	38. A	48. C
9. C	19. B	29. C	39. B	49. B
10. D	20. A	30. B	40. D	50. B

TEST 2

DIRECTIONS: Each question or incomplete statement is followed by several suggested answers or completions. Select the one that BEST answers the question or completes the statement. *PRINT THE LETTER OF THE CORRECT ANSWER IN THE SPACE AT THE RIGHT.*

1. A certain food is sold in 4 ounce cans at 10 for $3.00 and in 1 pound cans at 3 for $3.00. The SAVINGS in price per ounce by purchasing the food in the larger can is _____ cents/ounce.

    A. 1.59 B. 1.05 C. 1.25 D. 2.04

    1.____

2. After an article is discounted at 25%, it sells for $375. The ORIGINAL price of the article was

    A. $93.75 B. $350 C. $375 D. $500

    2.____

3. Assume that you require 1440 pencils, packed 12 to the box, 24 boxes to the carton. Which of the following represents the LOWEST bid for these pencils?

    A. 20¢ per pencil
    B. $65.00 per carton
    C. $2.70 per box less a 4% discount
    D. $400 less a 3% discount

    3.____

4. If erasers cost 8¢ each for the first 250, 7¢ each for the next 250, and 5¢ for every eraser thereafter, how many erasers may be purchased for $50?

    A. 600 B. 750 C. 850 D. 1000

    4.____

5. Assume that a buyer saves $14 on the purchase of an item that is discounted at 25%. The amount of money that the buyer must pay for the item is

    A. $42 B. $52 C. $54 D. $56

    5.____

Questions 6-9.

DIRECTIONS: Questions 6 through 9 are based on the following method of obtaining a reorder point: multiply the monthly rate of consumption by the lead time (in months) and add the minimum balance.

6. If the lead time is one-half month, the minimum balance is 6 units, and the monthly rate of consumption is 4 units, then the reorder point is _____ units.

    A. 4 B. 6 C. 8 D. 12

    6.____

7. If the reorder point is 25 units, the lead time is 3 months, and the minimum balance is 10 units, then the average monthly rate of consumption is _____ units.

    A. 3 B. 5 C. 6 D. 10

    7.____

8. If the reorder point is 400 units, the lead time is 2 months, and the monthly rate of consumption is 150 units, then the minimum balance is _____ units.

    A. 50 B. 100 C. 150 D. 200

    8.____

9. If the reorder point is 75 units, the monthly rate of consumption is 60 units, and the minimum balance is 45 units, then the lead time is _____ month(s).

   A. $\frac{1}{2}$ B. 1   C. 2   D. 4

10. A purchasing office has 4,992 special requisitions to be processed. Working alone, Buyer A could process these in 30 days; working alone, Buyer B could process these in 40 days; working alone, Buyer C could process these in 60 days.
    The LEAST number of days in which Buyers A, B, and C working together can process these 4,992 special requisitions is APPROXIMATELY _____ days.

    A. 14   B. 20   C. 34   D. 45

11. In MOST large manufacturing plants, quality control is a function of the

    A. accounting department
    B. executive staff
    C. personnel department
    D. production department

12. *Net weight* refers to the weight of

    A. an article exclusive of the weights of all packing materials and containers
    B. the shipment at time of packaging including weight of container
    C. the total amount ordered including that which is back-ordered
    D. the total load including all packaging material containers

13. *Invoice* may BEST be defined as

    A. buyer's statement of quantities of merchandise and prices to be furnished by the seller
    B. purchaser's written offer to a supplier formally stating all terms and conditions of a proposed transaction
    C. seller's itemized bill stating prices and quantities of goods delivered and sent to the buyer for payment
    D. sales agreement granting purchaser any discount established by the seller prior to the shipment date

14. Reclaimed property which can be repaired or reused in another manner is MOST likely to be classified as

    A. excess   B. obsolete   C. salvage   D. scrap

15. In preparing specifications for bond and ledger paper, the LEAST important item to be included is

    A. conformity to standards
    B. detailed manufacturing processes
    C. finish and surface
    D. size, weight, and color

16. The standard specifications has LEAST significance for

    A. encouraging substitute bids
    B. enabling the buyer to set quality standards when seeking bids
    C. helping using departments to prepare requisitions
    D. providing the testing laboratory with a basis for comparison of material submitted to it

Questions 17-20.

DIRECTIONS: Questions 17 through 20 refer to types of paper and a description of the quality of each. Match each type of paper in Column I with the appropriate description in Column II.

COLUMN I

17. Bond

18. Duplicator

19. Mimeograph

20. Offset

COLUMN II

A. Paper used primarily on printing presses

B. Paper with shiny hard surface which does not absorb alcohol well

C. Somewhat coarse in finish and absorbs ink well

D. Usually sulphite or rag content and used for correspondence

17.____
18.____
19.____
20.____

21. 1,000 sheets of Sub. 20 paper, size 17" x 22" weighs MOST NEARLY _____ pounds. 21.____

    A. 20   B. 40   C. 60   D. 80

22. In requisitions for lead pencils for general office use, the pencil numbers you should generally expect to appear MOST frequently are the numbers 22.____

    A. 1 and 6   B. 2 and 3   C. 2 and 5   D. 3 and 4

23. Of the following types of lead pencils, the number which represents the HARDEST lead is 23.____

    A. 2B   B. 2H   C. 3B   D. 9H

24. One pound (16 oz.) is equal to _____ grams. 24.____

    A. 100   B. 256   C. 454   D. 1,000

25. How many sheets are there in a ream of paper? 25.____

    A. 200   B. 500   C. 750   D. 1,000

26. The word *prototype* means a(n) 26.____

    A. design of type used in printing
    B. figure or symbol impressed in the manufacture of a product to identify the maker
    C. original or model
    D. method of typewriting

Questions 27-32.

DIRECTIONS: Each of Questions 27 through 32 consists of a statement which contains one word that is incorrectly used because it is not in keeping with the meaning that the quotation is intended to convey. Determine which word is incorrectly used. Then, select from the words lettered A, B, C, or D the word which, when substituted for the incorrectly used word, would BEST help to convey the meaning of the statement.

27. Determining compliance with the required quality is perhaps the most involved and probably one of the most important parts of a good quality-control program.
To function effectively, quality determination should be made immediately on use of the shipment

    A. after B. quantity C. receipt D. system

28. The bidders' list must be sufficient to ensure cooperation. Three is considered the practical minimum number of bidders when the product to be purchased is standardized or the specifications definitely established.
A greater number is desirable, even necessary, when alternates are to be considered, and particularly when specification recommendations are being sought.

    A. competition B. lesser
    C. small D. unique

29. Purchasing recommends flexibility in specifications to insure wide competition. It discourages the use of commercial standards and tolerances and recommends close adherence to, or allows room for, filling specifications with standard goods. These, of course, are less expensive and are readily available.
In this way, more vendors may be reached.

    A. distribution B. encourages
    C. industrial D. reliable

30. Purchasing will seek specifications, i.e., accurate descriptions of the material to be purchased, with few tolerances since unnecessary precision is costly.
Further, to permit competition, purchasing will recommend specifications which can be met by many vendors.

    A. absolute B. limit
    C. reasonable D. prices

31. Inventory turnover rates serve as useful guides in reducing inventories, effecting savings, and influencing procurement schedules.
Careful classification of inventory into perishable and permanent items is necessary after turnover rates are set.

    A. before B. helpful
    C. increasing D. non-perishable

32. Record keeping of materials in storage is closely associated with the purchasing of the materials. Coordinating stores keeping and purchasing obstructs effective inventory controls and economies.
The storage division can inform purchasing of turnover of items to prevent over- or under-stocking of materials.

    A. authorize B. combining
    C. loosely D. provides

Questions 33-45.

DIRECTIONS: For Questions 33 through 45, choose from the given classifications the one under which the item is MOST likely to be found in general stock catalogs.

33. *Chisels* may BEST be classified under

    A. food and condiments
    B. hand tools and accessories
    C. office machines and equipment
    D. stationery supplies

34. *Columnar pads* may BEST be classified under

    A. drygoods, textiles, and floor covering
    B. hospital and surgical supplies
    C. recreational supplies and equipment
    D. stationery and office supplies

35. *Gingham* may BEST be classified under

    A. clothing and textiles
    B. hand tools
    C. lighting apparatus
    D. paints and paint ingredients

36. *Trowels* may BEST be classified under

    A. dry goods and textiles
    B. hand tools and agricultural implements
    C. household supplies
    D. surgical supplies

37. *Collanders* may BEST be classified under

    A. building materials
    B. kitchen utensils
    C. motor vehicle parts
    D. plumbing supplies

38. *Litmus paper* may BEST be classified under

    A. laboratory supplies
    B. sewing supplies
    C. stationery and supplies
    D. textiles

39. *Pipettes* may BEST be classified under

    A. hardware
    B. hospital and laboratory supplies
    C. kitchen utensils and tableware
    D. plumbing fixtures and parts

40. *Carbon tetrachloride* may BEST be classified under

    A. brushes
    B. clothing and textiles
    C. drugs and chemicals
    D. toilet articles and accessories

41. *Curry powder* may BEST be classified under

   A. drugs and chemicals
   B. food and condiments
   C. paints and supplies
   D. surgical and dental supplies

42. *Planes* may BEST be classified under

   A. floor coverings
   B. hand tools
   C. household utensils
   D. plumbing fixtures

43. *Wing nuts* may BEST be classified under

   A. food and condiments
   B. hardware supplies
   C. household utensils
   D. sewing supplies

44. *Chambray* may BEST be classified under

   A. canned goods, food and misc. groceries
   B. brooms and brushes
   C. drugs and chemicals
   D. dry goods and textiles

45. *Shears* may BEST be classified under

   A. agricultural implements
   B. clothing and textiles
   C. electrical parts
   D. furniture

46. A BASIC reason for assigning commodity code numbers to purchased and stored items is to

   A. prevent pilferage
   B. increase the use of mechanized equipment
   C. facilitate ready reference in communications
   D. decrease flexibility of storage areas

47. Which of the following is NOT an important reason for authorizing a purchasing department to control stores?

   A. Coordination of purchasing and stores may result in economies.
   B. Record keeping of materials in storage is closely associated with the purchase of materials.
   C. The storage division can inform purchasing of turnover of items to prevent overstocking or understocking.
   D. The storerooms will be near the points of use, reducing transportation costs.

48. Any food or drug found by the comptroller to be unwholesome or otherwise unfit for human consumption or use shall NOT be removed by the vendor until it has been examined by the

   A. department of purchase
   B. environmental protection administration
   C. municipal service administration
   D. department of health

49. Which one of the following is a major function of the board of standardization of the department of purchase? 49.____

    A. Determination of locations for major future capital expenditures
    B. Establishment of time limitations for the processing of vouchers for payment
    C. Review and approval of purchasing specifications
    D. Review of maximum floor load limitations in department of purchase storehouses

50. Which one of the following is LEAST likely to be a major commodity grouping utilized by a central purchasing agency? 50.____

    A. Automotive equipment and supplies
    B. Condiments and seasonings
    C. Foods, fresh and processed
    D. Fuels, lubricating and plumbing supplies

KEY (CORRECT ANSWERS)

1. C	11. D	21. B	31. A	41. B
2. D	12. A	22. B	32. D	42. B
3. A	13. C	23. D	33. B	43. B
4. B	14. C	24. C	34. D	44. D
5. A	15. B	25. B	35. A	45. A
6. C	16. A	26. C	36. B	46. C
7. B	17. D	27. C	37. B	47. D
8. B	18. B	28. A	38. A	48. D
9. A	19. C	29. B	39. B	49. C
10. A	20. A	30. C	40. C	50. B

EXAMINATION SECTION
TEST 1

DIRECTIONS: Each question or incomplete statement is followed by several suggested answers or completions. Select the one the BEST answers the question or completes the statement. *PRINT THE LETTER OF THE CORRECT ANSWER IN THE SPACE AT THE RIGHT.*

1. In submitting a request for bids, a buyer's specifications should be written in a way that　　1.____

    A. limits the ranges of tolerance as much as possible
    B. allows more than one supplier to be competitive
    C. allows multiple interpretations of what is desired
    D. guarantees one successful bid

2. An agency commissions a graphic arts firm to design a letterhead and print the official stationery for the agency. In order to insure that the agency itself holds ownership of the design of the letterhead, the buyer should be sure to include a(n) _____ clause in the purchase agreement.　　2.____

    A. severability
    B. hold harmless
    C. disclaimer
    D. work for hire

3. After receiving a bid from a supplier, a buyer decides to change some of the terms and conditions of the original request, and makes the changes on the purchase order. The purchase order, in terms of contract law, may now be considered a(n)　　3.____

    A. counteroffer
    B. acceptance
    C. offer
    D. consideration

4. A buyer has limited space available for inventory storage, and the supplier's goods are therefore delivered in small batches. To lower the purchasing costs, the buyer should try to　　4.____

    A. order from several different suppliers
    B. send a worker from the organization to pick up the supplies, since they are small-batch shipments, to eliminate shipping costs
    C. offer to store inventory on consignment
    D. order larger batches, but spread out delivery until needed and the time for payments at an appropriate interval after each delivery

5. A way bill is a　　5.____

    A. fee charged by the common carrier for the transport of goods
    B. list of goods sent by a common carrier with shipping directions
    C. specification of the weight of packaging or wrapping of a product
    D. written receipt given by a carrier for goods accepted for transportation

6. Which of the following methods of shipment is typically MOST expensive?

    A. Less truck load (LTL)
    B. Less rail carload
    C. Rail carload
    D. Truckload

7. "Budgetary quotations" from vendors

    A. are long-term projections
    B. do not represent a binding commitment
    C. should not be used at all in making cost estimates
    D. are a good tool for leveraging price reductions during negotiations

8. A supplier requests a price increase of 3% on a long-term materials purchasing agreement. In order to negotiate the request, the buyer should be keeping an accessible record of
    I. the date(s) of the supplier's last price increase(s) on the materials
    II. how much prices have changed over time for the materials
    III. the cost-of-living adjustment index over the given period of time
    IV. the purchasing organization's change in revenues over the given period of time

    A. I and II
    B. I, II and III
    C. III and IV
    D. I, II, III and IV

9. Each of the following is a reason organizations use purchase orders to document transactions, EXCEPT to

    A. help control administrative matters
    B. facilitate the management of purchasing functions
    C. eliminate the need to look up price histories
    D. provide legal protection for the buying organization

10. A buyer has decided to use sample testing as a quality assessment strategy for a supplier's goods. As a rule, the samples should be tested

    A. and then destroyed
    B. before they are shipped
    C. without the use of statistical methods
    D. randomly throughout the batch

11. Express warranties include each of the following, EXCEPT a supplier's

    A. unstated promise that the product is fit for the ordinary purposes for which it is used
    B. oral or written promise containing representations that the product is defect free and/or a promise to repair or replace it.
    C. written promise to repair or replace defective parts for a stated period of time. This is a typical Song Beverly express warranty.
    D. written promise or affirmation of fact which describes the product at the time of sale

12. A seller offers a buyer a discount that is stipulated "2 percent 10th prox." on the purchase order. This means that the buyer will receive the 2 percent discount if the invoice is paid

    A. within ten days
    B. before the end of the month
    C. on or before the 10th of the following month
    D. within six months

13. The _____ department at the buying organization typically checks to make certain the products received match the specifications of what was ordered and reports discrepancies.

    A. quality control
    B. accounting
    C. purchasing
    D. receiving

14. When carrying out the purchasing function, a buyer should think of the _____ as the customer.

    A. buyer himself/herself
    B. purchasing department
    C. purchasing organization that is paying for the product
    D. requestor or user of the product purchased

15. For most organizations, a _____ supply of commonly-used business forms is considered optimal, taking all factors into account.

    A. monthly   B. quarterly   C. six-month   D. yearly

16. The most commonly used term indicating the geographical point where ownership passes from the seller to the buyer is

    A. Free On Board
    B. Duty-free
    C. Free Along Side
    D. Point of Assumption

17. Ideally-except for unique items available only from one supplier-competitive quotations should be obtained

    A. every time an order is placed
    B. every six months
    C. annually
    D. every two years

18. The F.O.B. point specified in a purchase order determines

    A. the cost of insurance and freight during delivery
    B. the means by which purchased goods are transported
    C. who normally pays for transportation of purchased goods
    D. whether the purchased goods have been paid for

19. The object of a(n) _____ bill of lading is to enable a shipper to collect for his shipment before it reaches destination.

    A. order
    B. straight
    C. export
    D. foul

20. What is the term for an invoice sent by a supplier in advance of the actual sale for planning or other purposes?

    A. Traveler card
    B. Release
    C. Tickler
    D. Pro forma

21. When a purchasing agent arranges an order for long-term material needs, he should be sure to require a(n)

    A. flexible specification
    B. hold harmless clause
    C. supremacy clause
    D. sample shipment

22. In order to ensure prompt delivery of the material or service specified on a purchase order, a purchaser's best choice is to

    A. write "ASAP" as the delivery date
    B. specify the length of time in terms of days
    C. specify the length of time in terms of weeks
    D. specify the exact date by which the material will be delivered or the service completed

23. Of the categories of purchases used at a mid- to large-sized organization, the LEAST common is

    A. maintenance, repair, and operating supplies
    B. raw material
    C. items for resale
    D. capital equipment

24. A purchasing agent should typically expect to have the LEAST amount of authority in the purchase of

    A. MRO purchases
    B. consulting services
    C. revenue-producing items
    D. capital equipment

25. A buyer arranges a purchase agreement stating that the order will be shipped "C&F destination." This means that the   25.____

    A. supplier arranges for the insurance and charges the buyer
    B. supplier pays the F.O.B. costs
    C. buyer pays for the F.O.B costs
    D. buyer bills the supplier for transportation costs

KEY (CORRECT ANSWERS)

1.	B	11.	A
2.	D	12.	C
3.	A	13.	A
4.	D	14.	D
5.	B	15.	C
6.	A	16.	A
7.	B	17.	C
8.	A	18.	C
9.	C	19.	A
10.	D	20.	D

21. D
22. D
23. C
24. B
25. C

TEST 2

DIRECTIONS: Each question or incomplete statement is followed by several suggested answers or completions. Select the one the BEST answers the question or completes the statement. *PRINT THE LETTER OF THE CORRECT ANSWER IN THE SPACE AT THE RIGHT.*

1. The Last In First Out (LIFO) accounting method
    I. values inventory at current prices
    II. tends to postpone outlays for income taxes
    III. shows higher income than First In First Out (FIFO) if prices are rising

    A. I only
    B. I and II
    C. I and III
    D. II and III

2. Which of the following is an express warranty?

    A. "The delivered product will match the physical dimensions of the submitted sample."
    B. "This is the best computer available on the market today."
    C. "This truck gets great gas mileage."
    D. "I guarantee you'll be satisfied with this printer."

3. For routine supplies that are widely available, the most important purchasing cost factor, other than price, is probably

    A. required delivery date
    B. labor charges
    C. material quality
    D. shipping charges

4. Which of the following is a term frequently used in connection with bills of lading which are endorsed over to another party by the owner of the bill-giving the party named the title to the property covered by the bill of lading?

    A. Pledge
    B. Assignment
    C. Attachment
    D. Transference

5. A buyer writes "ASAP" on a purchase order in order to communicate the urgency of the supplier's delivery. The main problem with this approach is that it

    A. communicates a lack of planning and discipline on the part of the buyer's organization
    B. puts pressure on the supplier to meet an unrealistic deadline
    C. does not specify a specific date for delivery
    D. is an acronym that has multiple meanings

6. A supplier has negotiated "net terms" for a purchase. This means that

    A. the supplier's invoice must be paid without discount on or before the due date
    B. the buyer will only pay for what is delivered, when it is delivered
    C. the supplier will offer a discount if the buyer pays an invoice before the due date
    D. the buyer pays for everything up front

7. A company has purchased a machine for making envelopes. A week after it is put into operation, a bolt in the machine is sheared off and the broken end is flung several feet, injuring a worker in the eye. In order to arrange an agreement in which the supplier would assume liability for this injury, a buyer would probably have to delete the existing exclusion concerning

    A. consequential damages
    B. negotiable instruments
    C. implied warranty
    D. unconscionability

8. _____ is a term of quality concern that usually involves pre-packaged, off-the-shelf items.

    A. Planned obsolescence
    B. In-process checking
    C. Concealed discrepancy
    D. Tare deduction

9. Which of the following is an advantage typically associated with the use of procurement cards among an organization's employees?

    A. Tight control over number and type of purchases
    B. Lower overall cost of the purchasing function
    C. Strengthened negotiating position
    D. Savings in paperwork and time

10. The theory of "first bid, final bid" is that
    I. a supplier will keep the price as low as possible
    II. a supplier will make the terms as favorable as possible
    III. the buyer will save time
    IV. the buyer will have maximum flexibility in choosing terms and price

    A. I and II
    B. I, II and III
    C. II and IV
    D. I, II, III and IV

11. An implied warranty of merchantability is the implicit promise that a product will be

    A. fit for the ordinary purposes for which it is used
    B. similar or identical to the products of its competitors
    C. fit for the particular purpose specified by the buyer
    D. repaired or replaced, if defective, within a reasonable period of time

12. The price of a product is $45. The supplier wants to increase the price to $50, but the purchasing agent convinces the supplier to keep the price the same. The percentage saved by the agent was

    A. 10
    B. 11.1
    C. 15
    D. 22.33

13. A buyer for a local government office purchases Brand X paint for the building's interior rooms at the lowest available price, which is $5 a gallon less than the nearest competitor, Brand A. Which of the following, if true, would have been a legitimate reason for the buyer to decide on buying Brand A?

    A. The agency only planned to occupy the building for a year or so
    B. The application of Brand A costs slightly more than applying Brand X
    C. Other agencies have used Brand A for their offices and have had no complaints
    D. Brand A is twice as durable as Brand X

14. "External lead-time" includes the time required for the
    I. supplier to manufacture the ordered material
    II. carrier to transport the ordered material
    III. purchaser to inspect the quality of the goods upon arrival
    IV. purchaser to deliver the material to the requestor

    A. I only
    B. I and II
    C. III and IV
    D. I, II, III and IV

15. The portion of law that is concerned with the scope of a buyer's or purchaser's authority is known as the Law of

    A. Agency
    B. Torts
    C. Contract
    D. Partnership

16. Inputs into a material requirements planning (MRP) system include each of the following, EXCEPT

    A. holding costs
    B. lead times
    C. bills of materials
    D. production schedule

17. Often, a long-term agreement between a buyer and supplier does not specify on the purchase order form what quantity to ship at any one time, or the dates that shipment should be made. The mechanism for ordering in this type of arrangement is the

    A. invoice
    B. release form
    C. traveler card
    D. pro forma

18. Most of the disputes concerning orders for long-term material needs arise because 18.____

    A. turnover at the supplier's workplace is high
    B. manufacturing standards constantly evolve
    C. the definition of acceptability is too vague
    D. the purchasing organization hasn't maintained adequate records

19. For a purchasing company that is experiencing habitually late shipments from its suppliers, the least costly solution is likely to be 19.____

    A. ordering material from multiple suppliers
    B. carrying high inventory
    C. multiple follow-ups with a supplier or shipper
    D. implementing a just-in-time purchasing arrangement

20. To gain a price reduction from a supplier, a purchasing agent's FIRST step should be to 20.____

    A. threaten to change suppliers
    B. offer to pay cash
    C. offer to accept a later delivery schedule
    D. ask the supplier to lower the price

21. The _____ department at the buying organization typically matches invoices to the purchase order to make certain that prices, terms, and the quantities and items received agree before payment is approved. 21.____

    A. purchasing   B. receiving
    C. quality control   D. accounting

22. For _____, the best purchasing approach is usually to keep as little as possible on hand. 22.____

    A. revenue-producing items
    B. office supplies
    C. capital expenditures
    D. printed forms

23. In international trade, a seller often agrees to deliver the product to a specified port for ocean shipping. Afterwards the buyer pays for the cost of loading, marine insurance, and further transportation costs. This type of agreement is described as 23.____

    A. Forward Buying   B. Tare Free
    C. Free Along Side   D. Free On Board

24. An Economic Order Quantity (EOQ) formula would be an appropriate inventory method for 24.____

    A. consulting services   B. machines used in production
    C. office supplies   D. fleet vehicles

25. Relative to financing a purchase, leasing typically has the advantage of
    I. greater flexibility
    II. fewer financial restrictions
    III. lower overall costs
    IV. full control over the leased item

    A. I and II
    B. I, II and III
    C. II and III
    D. I, II, III and IV

KEY (CORRECT ANSWERS)

1. B
2. A
3. A
4. B
5. C

6. A
7. A
8. C
9. D
10. B

11. A
12. B
13. D
14. B
15. A

16. A
17. B
18. C
19. D
20. D

21. D
22. A
23. C
24. C
25. A

EXAMINATION SECTION
TEST 1

DIRECTIONS: Each question or incomplete statement is followed by several suggested answers or completions. Select the one the BEST answers the question or completes the statement. *PRINT THE LETTER OF THE CORRECT ANSWER IN THE SPACE AT THE RIGHT.*

1. A purchase order must include the
    I. name and address of the supplier
    II. payment terms
    III. quantity of goods/services purchases
    IV. location where the buyer will take ownership

    A. I and III
    B. I, II and III
    C. II and III
    D. I, II, III and IV

    1.____

2. Typically, ownership referred to as "title of goods" is transferred from seller to buyer when

    A. initial payment for the goods has been made
    B. the goods are transferred from seller to buyer at the agreed-upon point of delivery
    C. final payment for the goods has been made
    D. the title document is delivered to the buyer from the seller

    2.____

3. Team-buying arrangements are usually MOST appropriate for transactions that are

    A. low-value and routine
    B. low-value and one-time
    C. high-value and one-time
    D. high-value and continuous

    3.____

4. A(n) _____ bill of lading is a nonnegotiable document and provides that a shipment is to be delivered direct to the party whose name is shown as consignee.

    A. foul
    B. straight
    C. order
    D. clean

    4.____

5. What is the term for the process of notifying a buyer that an offer or purchase order has been received?

    A. Exchange
    B. Consideration
    C. Substantiation
    D. Acknowledgement

    5.____

2 (#1)

6. Effective methods of cutting down on office supply expenses generally include
   I. standardizing products
   II. allow sales personnel to call on each office employee individually to determine need
   III. use a systems contract
   IV. have supplies located at several different locations throughout the workplace

   A. I only
   B. I and III
   C. II, III and IV
   D. IV only

7. A seller offers a buyer a discount that is stipulated "2 percent 1-60X" on the purchase order. This means the buyer will receive the 2 percent discount if the invoice is paid within _____ days of the delivery date.

   A. 60
   B. 70
   C. 90
   D. 121

8. A business that transports goods by motor vehicle to a customer and agrees to accept certain terms and conditions is known specifically as a

   A. contract carrier
   B. freight company
   C. common carrier
   D. bailor

9. A "traveler card" in a purchasing office is a type of

   A. purchase order
   B. price history
   C. release form
   D. requisition fo

10. In evaluating the quality of a vendor, the most important factor is probably

    A. whether the vendor prefers a purchase order or a contract
    B. how the vendor reacts to problems
    C. price
    D. an absence of problems

11. Probably the most important factor in the success of purchasing efforts is the

    A. clarity of delivery date
    B. lead-time involved
    C. calculation of price
    D. quality of specifications

12. Buyers at an organization are normally considered to be _____ purchasing agents.

    A. universal   B. general   C. principal   D. special

13. In order to function more smoothly with other departments in an organization, such as receiving, purchasing should network its computer system. Usually, it would be appropriate for receiving to have access to information about each of the following, EXCEPT

   A. delivery dates
   B. price information
   C. F.O.B. points
   D. invoice dates

14. "Safety stock" is added inventory that is meant to insure against each of the following, EXCEPT

   A. a sales bubble
   B. unexpected lead time
   C. fluctuating rates of usage
   D. obsolescence, failure, or breakage

15. For a printing project, the most efficient way to specify the organization's needs is to

   A. rely on standard procedures
   B. request a number of samples
   C. provide a sample
   D. provide a bulleted list of extremely narrow requirements

16. In larger organizations, the _____ is usually established outside of the purchasing operation.

   A. request for bids
   B. request for bids
   C. maximum price
   D. need for materials or services
   E. confirmation of orders

17. Which of the following methods of shipment is typically LEAST expensive?

   A. Truckload
   B. Rail carload
   C. Less truckload (LTL)
   D. Less carload

18. What is the term for the document used on foreign trade that requires payment by the seller's bank for a shipment when the document is presented and accompanied by any agreed-upon proof of shipment?

   A. FOB
   B. Letter of credit
   C. Pro forma
   D. Sight draft

19. The most appropriate office software for bid analysis is the

   A. slide presentation
   B. expert system
   C. spreadsheet
   D. financial planner

20. For a buyer, the <u>first</u> step in quality assurance is usually

   A. making a thorough inspection of a product as soon as it is shipped
   B. communicating the importance of meeting the given standards
   C. obtaining a variety of samples
   D. writing good specifications

21. Items that are used internally in a business or organization are often abbreviated _____ on purchasing documents.

   A. ISO
   B. FOB
   C. LCL
   D. MRO

22. The economic order quantity (EOQ) of an item depends on each of the following factors, EXCEPT

   A. unit demand
   B. quantity price breaks
   C. holding costs
   D. costs of being out of inventory

23. Which of the following is most clearly a breach of the implied warranty of fitness for a particular purpose?

   A. The lead of a pencil, just delivered by a supplier, breaks every time an office worker puts it to paper.
   B. The paint that a buyer recently purchased, one month after being properly applied by a contractor, is peeling from the walls.
   C. A metal machine component is .025 of an inch longer than allowed by the specifications of a purchase order.
   D. Reams of paper delivered by the supplier are slightly too large to fit into the paper tray of the copy machine for which they were intended.

24. A supplier tries to change the terms of an agreement at the last minute by adjusting the price upward. The buyer's right to _____ allows him to purchase goods from another source and obtain any difference in price from the original supplier.

   A. cover
   B. exemption
   C. recourse
   D. utility

25. A retail store sells equal amounts of a product over a five-month period, beginning in January, at a 100% markup. The company's annual interest rate is 10 percent. The most efficient purchasing structure would be to

    A. buy all the products up front in a lump purchase
    B. use weekly sales to predict quantity, and then place orders
    C. spread purchases out in five equal monthly amounts
    D. buy all the products up front in a lump purchase, but divide the deliv-

25.____

KEY (CORRECT ANSWERS)

1.	D	11.	D
2.	B	12.	B
3.	D	13.	B
4.	B	14.	D
5.	D	15.	C
6.	B	16.	C
7.	B	17.	B
8.	A	18.	D
9.	D	19.	C
10.	B	20.	B

21. D
22. B
23. B
24. A
25. D

TEST 2

DIRECTIONS: Each question or incomplete statement is followed by several suggested answers or completions. Select the one the BEST answers the question or completes the statement. *PRINT THE LETTER OF THE CORRECT ANSWER IN THE SPACE AT THE RIGHT.*

1. In predicting prices, a buyer should rely LEAST on

   A. trends
   B. budgets
   C. vendor communication
   D. experience

2. The main advantage of an operating lease is that it

   A. can be converted into ownership cheaply and quickly
   B. does not have to be entered on the balance sheet as a liability
   C. they are inherently unstructured
   D. reduces overall acquisition costs

3. The Economic Order Quantity formula takes each of the following into account, EXCEPT

   A. price
   B. obsolescence
   C. the holding cost of inventory
   D. the cost of placing an order

4. A purchasing agent's activity report will usually contain each of the following, EXCEPT

   A. impending strikes
   B. major price increases or reductions
   C. current lead times for certain items
   D. unresolved claims for damaged material

5. The bill of lading is a

   A. written receipt given by a carrier for goods accepted for transportation
   B. fee charged by a government for certain goods brought into the country
   C. purchase order for materials or supplies used over an extended period of time
   D. list of goods sent by a common carrier with shipping directions

6. Which of the following federal agencies compiles the Producer Price Index (PPI)?

   A. Small Business Administration
   B. Bureau of Economic Analysis
   C. Bureau of Labor Statistics
   D. Patent and Trademark Office

7. A request for quotation (RFQ) should
   I. give the names of all competitors
   II. avoid language such as "evaluate the feasibility" or "reserves the right to"
   III. identify the estimated annual purchases of the expense category
   IV. always be in writing

A. I and III
B. II and III
C. II, III and IV
D. I, II, III and IV

8. Probably the major reason for failed negotiations with a potential supplier is that the buyer

   A. doesn't allow sufficient time to reach an agreement
   B. technology changes rapidly
   C. isn't willing to offer endorsements up-front
   D. has not adequately planned for negotiations

8.____

9. Sellers may disclaim the implied warranty of merchantability by using the
   I. word "merchantability" in the disclaimer, and writing the disclaimer itself conspicuously (in larger type or ALL CAPITALS, etc.)
   II. phrase "as is"
   III. phrase "with all faults"
   IV. phrase "not for resale"

   A. I and II
   B. I, II and III
   C. II and III
   D. I, II, III and IV

9.____

10. For a buyer, the most accurate way to think of "price" would be to view it as

    A. the final determining factor in all purchasing decisions
    B. a dependent variable that changes in relation to factors such as delivery time, quality, and warranties
    C. one component of cost, but not necessarily the most important
    D. a margin over cost that is passed on to the purchasing company's customers

10.____

11. "Dating" is a method of

    A. granting extended credit terms used by sellers to induce buyers to receive goods in advance of their required delivery date, thus permitting the seller to ship goods earlier than the buyer would ordinarily wish to receive them
    B. stipulating that the price of the goods ordered is subject to change at the vendor's discretion between the date the order is placed and the date the vendor makes shipment, and that the then established price is the contract price
    C. debiting delays in excess of the allowed free time provided in tariffs against the consignor (or consignee), and crediting delays less than those allowed to the consignor (or consignee)
    D. withholding a portion of the sum due a vendor until the purchase has been finally accepted as fully meeting specifications

11.____

12. A buyer has a relationship with a supplier that is on an order-by-order basis, with no special provisions about price increases in the contract. The supplier announces a price increase. The buyer knows that the cost of switching to another supplier will probably equal, if not exceed, the cost of the price increase. The buyer should

12.____

A. threaten to open the contract up for competitive bidding
B. offer to buy a larger quantity of items in order to lower the price
C. ask the supplier for a 90-day postponement for budget adjustment
D. threaten to make a contract with the supplier's leading competitor

13. In analyzing a group of bids, a buyer's should think of his/her primary responsibility as

A. locating hidden costs
B. finding the lowest possible price
C. converting price information into cost information
D. avoiding any kind of risk

14. In negotiation with a supplier, a buyer for Agency X makes the statement that Agency X is already receiving a product offered by a supplier for a lower price from another supplier. The supplier challenges the buyer's statement in court, and the buyer is unable to prove that his statement was correct. The buyer is in violation of _____ law.

A. labor
B. false advertising
C. antitrust
D. trade secrecy

15. Which of the following terms is synonymous with "equity?"

A. Book value
B. Deferred revenue
C. Asset turnover
D. Future value

16. Hard copies of bills of material usually include
   I. the name of the supplier
   II. the quantity needed
   III. the price previously paid for the material
   IV. a brief description of the item needed

A. I and II
B. I, II and III
C. II and IV
D. I, II, III and IV

17. A buyer wants to ensure that quality assurance is an issue that is important to a supplier. Before the buyer even enters into an agreement with a supplier, the best way to do this would be to

A. write very narrow specifications
B. request a description of the supplier's own quality assurance policies and protocols
C. reiterate several times, on several occasions, that quality assurance is important to the long-term life of the purchasing agreement
D. make a list of qualities or characteristics that will be considered unacceptable

18. In order for a contract to be legal,
    I. the agreement must involve legal subject matter
    II. there must be an offer
    III. there must be an acceptance
    IV. parties to the agreement must be capable

    A. I and III
    B. I, II and III
    C. II, III and IV
    D. I, II, III and IV

    18.____

19. A buyer issues a purchase order for certain office supplies at a certain price that she believes was agreed upon by the supplier. The supplier does not agree with the price that is listed on the purchase order. Under contract law, the supplier has a period of _____ days from the receipt of the written purchase order to voice an objection.

    A. 5
    B. 10
    C. 30
    D. 60

    19.____

20. The "Just in Time" ordering method is best suited to organizations that

    A. provide services that are dependent on the prompt arrival of certain supplies
    B. have sales marked by pronounced boom-and-bust cycles
    C. works with informal procedures
    D. use standard products on a continual basis for an extended period of time

    20.____

21. The _____ department at the buying organization typically compares purchase order items and quantities with the physical items received and reports any discrepancies.

    A. accounting
    B. receiving
    C. purchasing
    D. quality control

    21.____

22. Advantages of multiple sourcing include
    I. less time spent on the purchasing function
    II. overall cost reduction
    III. protection against poor performance by a supplier
    IV. flexible specifications

    A. I and II
    B. II, III and IV
    C. III only
    D. I, II, III and IV

    22.____

23. Many buyers try to ensure the success of a purchasing agreement by writing specifications that are as narrow as possible. The greatest risk associated with this strategy is that

    A. it nearly always results in added fees or charges
    B. the availability of the named items may be limited
    C. the item is often too narrowly defined to fit the intended purpose
    D. other products that may satisfy the need at lower cost are excluded

    23.____

24. A purchasing agent orders a list of supplies from a large producer of metal products. The purchase includes several pressed metal sheets that will be used in manufacturing parts for resale. The supplier's invoice includes the same rate of sales tax for all the goods listed on the invoice. The purchasing agent should know that

   A. before the sheets can be purchased, they must be approved by the CPSC
   B. most states do not apply sales taxes to raw materials used in the manufacture of products for resale.
   C. the transformation of the metal sheets into a final product will require certain skills and machinery
   D. it is the purchasing organization's responsibility to ensure that the metal sheets are produced under OSHA-approved conditions

25. "Consideration" is a term in contract law that refers to the

   A. process of notifying a buyer that an offer or purchase order has been received
   B. careful inspection of the words of a contract, to make sure it says what each party wants it to
   C. giving of something-usually money-in exchange for goods or services
   D. fairness and rightness of conduct or action, given the circumstances

KEY (CORRECT ANSWERS)

1. A	11. A
2. B	12. C
3. B	13. C
4. C	14. C
5. A	15. A
6. C	16. C
7. D	17. B
8. D	18. D
9. B	19. B
10. C	20. D

21. B
22. C
23. D
24. B
25. C

EXAMINATION SECTION
TEST 1

DIRECTIONS: Each question or incomplete statement is followed by several suggested answers or completions. Select the one that BEST answers the question or completes the statement. *PRINT THE LETTER OF THE CORRECT ANSWER IN THE SPACE AT THE RIGHT.*

1. As a supervisor in a bureau, you have been asked by the head of the bureau to recommend whether or not the work of the bureau requires an increase in the permanent staff of the bureau.
   Of the following questions, the one whose answer would MOST likely assist you in making your recommendation is: Are
   A. some permanent employees working irregular hours because they occasionally work overtime?
   B. the present permanent employees satisfied with their work assignment?
   C. temporary employees hired to handle seasonal fluctuations in work load?
   D. the present permanent employees keeping the work of the bureau current?

   1.____

2. In making job assignments to his subordinates, a supervisor should follow the principle that each individual GENERALLY is capable of
   A. performing one type of work well and less capable of performing other types well
   B. learning to perform a wide variety of different types of work
   C. performing best the type of work in which he has had experience
   D. learning to perform any type of work in which he is given training

   2.____

3. Assume that you are the supervisor of a large number of clerks in a unit in a city agency. Your unit has just been given an important assignment which must be completed a week from now. You know that, henceforth, your unit will be given this assignment every six months.
   You or any one of your subordinates who has been properly instructed can complete this assignment in one day. This assignment is of a routine type which is ordinarily handled by clerks. There is enough time for you to train one of your subordinates to handle the assignment and then have him do it. However, it would take twice as much time for you to take this course of action as it would for you to do the assignment yourself.
   The one of the following courses of action which you should take in this situation is to
   A. do the assignment yourself as soon as possible without discussing it with any of your subordinates at this time
   B. do the assignment yourself and then train one of your subordinates to handle it in the future
   C. give the assignment to one of your subordinates after training him to handle it
   D. train each of your subordinates to do the assignment on a rotating basis after you have done it yourself the first time

   3.____

4. You are in charge of an office in which each member of the staff has a different set of duties, although each has the same title. No member of the staff can perform the duties of any other member of the staff without first receiving extensive training. Assume that it is necessary for one member of the staff to take on, in addition to his regular work, an assignment which any member of the staff is capable of carrying out.
The one of the following considerations which would have the MOST weight in determining which staff member is to be given the additional assignment is the
   A. quality of the work performed by the individual members of the staff
   B. time consumed by individual members of the staff in performing their work
   C. level of difficulty of the duties being performed by individual members of the staff
   D. relative importance of the duties being performed by individual members of the staff

5. The one of the following causes of clerical error which is usually considered to be LEAST attributable to faulty supervision or inefficient management is
   A. inability to carry out instructions
   B. too much work to do
   C. an inappropriate recordkeeping system
   D. continual interruptions

6. Suppose you are in charge of a large unit in which all of the clerical staff perform similar tasks.
In evaluating the relative accuracy of the clerks, the clerk who should be considered to be the LEAST accurate is the one
   A. whose errors result in the greatest financial loss
   B. whose errors cost the most to locate
   C. who makes the greatest percentage of errors in his work
   D. who makes the greatest number of errors in the unit

7. Assume that under a proposed procedure for handling employee grievances in a public agency, the first step to be taken is for the aggrieved employee to submit his grievance as soon as it arises to a grievance board set up to hear all employee grievances in the agency. The board, which is to consist of representatives of management and of rank and file employees, is to consider the grievance, obtain all necessary pertinent information, and then render a decision on the matter. Thus, the first-line supervisor would not be involved in the settlement of any of his subordinates' grievances except when asked by the board to submit information.
This proposed procedure would be generally UNDESIRABLE chiefly because the
   A. board may become a bottleneck to delay the prompt disposition of grievances
   B. aggrieved employees and their supervisors have not been first given the opportunity to resolve the grievances themselves

3 (#1)

C. employees would be likely to submit imaginary, as well as real, grievances to the board
D. board will lack first-hand, personal knowledge of the factors involved in grievances

8. Sometimes jobs in private organizations and public agencies are broken down so as to permit a high degree of job specialization.
Of the following, an IMPORTANT effect of a high degree of job specialization in a public agency is that employees performing
   A. highly specialized jobs may not be readily transferable to other jobs in the agency
   B. similar duties may require closer supervision than employees performing unrelated functions
   C. specialized duties can be held responsible for their work to a greater extent than can employees performing a wide variety of functions
   D. specialized duties will tend to cooperate readily with employees performing other types of specialized duties

8.____

9. Assume that you are the supervisor of a clerical unit in an agency. One of your subordinates violates a rule of the agency, a violation which requires that the employee be suspended from his work for one day. The violated rule is one that you have found to be unduly strict, and you have recommended to the management of agency that the rule be changed or abolished. The management has been considering your recommendation but has not yet reached a decision on the matter.
In these circumstances, you should
   A. not initiate disciplinary action but, instead, explain to the employee that the rule may be changed shortly
   B. delay disciplinary action on the violation until the management has reached a decision on changing the rule
   C. modify the disciplinary action by reprimanding the employee and informing him that further action may be taken when the management has reached a decision on changing the rule
   D. initiate the prescribed disciplinary action with commenting on the strictness of the rule or on your recommendation

9.____

10. Assume that a supervisor praises his subordinates for satisfactory aspects of their work only when he is about to criticize them for unsatisfactory aspects of their work.
Such a practice is UNDESIRABLE primarily because
   A. his subordinates may expect to be praised for their work even if it is unsatisfactory
   B. praising his subordinates for some aspects of their work while criticizing other aspects will weaken the effects of the criticisms
   C. his subordinates would be more receptive to criticism if it were followed by praise
   D. his subordinates may come to disregard praise and wait for criticism to be given

10.____

11. The one of the following which would be the BEST reason for an agency to eliminate a procedure for obtaining and recording certain information is that
    A. it is no longer legally required to obtain the information
    B. there is no advantage in obtaining the information
    C. the information could be compiled on the basis of other information available
    D. the information obtained is sometimes incorrect

12. In determining the type and number of records to be kept in an agency, it is important to recognize that records are of value PRIMARILY as
    A. raw material to be used in statistical analysis
    B. sources of information about the agency's activities
    C. by-products of the activities carried on by the agency
    D. data for evaluating the effectiveness of the agency

13. Aside from requirements imposed by authority, the frequency with which reports are submitted or the length of the interval which they cover should depend PRINCIPALLY on the
    A. availability of the data to be included in the reports
    B. amount of time required to prepare the reports
    C. extent of the variations in the data with the passage of time
    D. degree of comprehensiveness required in the reports

14. Organizations that occupy large, general, open-area offices sometimes consider it desirable to build private offices for the supervisors of large bureaus. The one of the following which is generally NOT considered to be a justification of the use of private office is that they
    A. lend prestige to the person occupying the office
    B. provide facilities for private conferences
    C. achieve the maximum use of office space
    D. provide facilities for performing work requiring a high degree of concentration

15. The LEAST important factor to be considered in planning the layout of an office is the
    A. relative importance of the different types of work to be done
    B. convenience with which communication can be achieved
    C. functional relationships of the activities of the office
    D. necessity for screening confidential activities from unauthorized persons

16. The one of the following which is generally considered to be the CHIEF advantage of using data processing equipment in modern offices is to
    A. facilitate the use of a wide variety of sources of information
    B. supply management with current information quickly
    C. provide uniformity in the processing and reporting of information
    D. broaden the area in which management decisions can be made

17. In the box design of office forms, the spaces in which information is to be entered are arranged in boxes containing captions.
Of the following, the one which is generally NOT considered to be an acceptable rule in employing box design is that
    A. space should be allowed for the lengthiest anticipated entry in a box
    B. the caption should be located in the upper left corner of the box
    C. the boxes on a form should be of the same size and shape
    D. boxes should be aligned vertically whenever possible

17.____

18. As a management tool, the work count would generally be of LEAST assistance to a unit supervisor in
    A. scheduling the work of his unit
    B. locating bottlenecks in the work of his unit
    C. ascertaining the number of subordinates he needs
    D. tracing the flow of work in the unit

18.____

19. Of the following, the FIRST step that should be taken in a forms simplification program is to make a
    A. detailed analysis of the items found on current forms
    B. study of the amount of use made of existing forms
    C. survey of the amount of each kid of form on hand
    D. survey of the characteristics of the more effective forms in use

19.____

20. The work-distribution chart is a valuable tool for an office supervisor to use in conducting work simplification programs.
Of the following questions, the one which a work-distribution chart would generally be LEAST useful in answering is:
    A. What activities take the most time?
    B. Are the employees doing many unrelated tasks?
    C. Is work being distributed evenly among the employees?
    D. Are activities being performed in proper sequence?

20.____

21. Assume that, as a supervisor, you conduct, from time to time, work-performance studies in various sections of your agency. The units of measurement used in any study depend on the particular study and may be number of letters typed, number of papers filed, or other suitable units.
It is MOST important that the units of measurement to be used in a study conform to the units used in similar past studies when the
    A. units of measurement to be used in the study cannot be defined sharply
    B. units of measurement used in past studies were satisfactory
    C results of the study are to be compared with those of past studies
    D. results of the study are to be used for the same purpose as were those of past studies

21.____

22. As it is used in auditing, an internal check is a
    A. procedure which is designed to guard against fraud
    B. periodic audit by a public accounting firm to verify the accuracy of the internal transactions of an organization

22.____

C. document transferring funds from one section to another within an organization
D. practice of checking documents twice before they are transmitted outside an organization

23. Of the following, the one which can LEAST be considered to be a proper function of an accounting system is to
    A. indicate the need to curtail expenditures
    B. provide information for future fiscal programs
    C. record the expenditure of funds from special appropriations
    D. suggest method to expedite the collection of revenues

24. Assume that a new unit is to be established in an agency. The unit is to compile and tabulate data so that it will be of the greatest usefulness to the high-level administrators in the agency in making administrative decisions.
    In planning the organization of this unit, the question that should be answered FIRST is:
    A. What interpretations are likely to be made of the data by the high-level administrators in making decisions?
    B. At what point in the decision-making process will it be most useful to inject the data?
    C. What types of data will be required by high-level administrators in making decisions?
    D. What criteria will the high-level administrators use to evaluate the decisions they make?

25. The one of the following which is the CHIEF limitation of the organization chart as it is generally used in business and government is that the chart
    A. engenders within incumbents feelings of rights to positions they occupy
    B. reveals only formal authority relationships, omitting the informal ones
    C. shows varying degrees of authority even though authority is not subject to such differentiation
    D. presents organizational structure as it is rather than what it is supposed to be

26. The degree of decentralization that is effective and economical in an organization tends to vary INVERSELY with the
    A. size of the organization
    B. availability of adequate numbers of competent personnel
    C. physical dispersion of the organization's activities
    D. adequacy of the organization's communications system

27. The one of the following which usually can LEAST be considered to be an advantage of committees as they are generally used in government and business is that they
    A. provide opportunities for reconciling varying points of view
    B. promote coordination by the interchange of information among the members of the committee

C. act promptly in situations requiring immediate action
D. use group judgment to resolve questions requiring a wide range of experience

28. Managerial decentralization is defined as the decentralization of decision-making authority.
    The degree of managerial decentralization in an organization varies INVERSELY with the
    A. number of decisions made lower down the managerial hierarchy
    B. importance of the decisions made lower down the management hierarchy
    C. number of major organizational functions affected by decisions made at lower management levels
    D. amount of review to which decisions made at lower management levels are subjected

29. Some policy-making commissions are composed of members who are appointed to overlapping terms.
    Of the following, the CHIEF advantage of appointing members to overlapping terms in such commissions is that
    A. continuity of policy is promoted
    B. the likelihood of compromise policy decisions is reduced
    C. responsibility for policy decisions can be fixed upon individual members
    D. the likelihood of unanimity of opinion is increased

30. If a certain public agency with a fixed number of employees has a line organizational structure, then the width of the span of supervision is
    A. *inversely* proportional to the length of the chain of command in the organization
    B. *directly* proportional to the complexity of tasks performed in the organization
    C. *inversely* proportional to the competence of the personnel in the organization
    D. *directly* proportional to the number of levels of supervision existing in the organization

31. Mr. Brown is a supervisor in charge of a section of clerical employees in an agency. The section consists of four units, each headed by a unit supervisor. From time to time, he makes tours of his section for the purpose of maintaining contact with the rank and file employees. During these tours, he discusses with these employees their work production, work methods, work problems, and other related topics. The information he obtains in this manner is often incomplete or inaccurate. At meeting with the unit supervisors, he questions them on the information acquired during his tours. The supervisors are often unable to answer the questions immediately because they are based on incomplete or inaccurate information. When the supervisors ask that they be permitted to accompany Mr. Brown on his tours and thus answer his questions on the spot, Mr. Brown refuses, explaining that a rank and file employee might be reluctant to speak freely in the presence of his supervisor.

This situation may BEST be described as a violation of the principle of organization called
A. span of control
B. delegation of authority
C. specialization of work
D. unity of command

Questions 32-36.

DIRECTIONS: Each of Questions 32 through 36 consists of a statement which contains one word that is incorrectly used because it is not in keeping with the meaning that the quotation is evidently intended to convey. For each of these questions, you are to select the INCORRECTLY used word and substitute for it one of the word lettered A, B, C, or D, which helps BEST to convey the meaning of the statement.

32. There has developed in recent years an increasing awareness of the need to measure the quality of management in all enterprise and to seek the principles that can serve as a basis for this improvement.
A. growth
B. raise
C. efficiency
D. define

33. It is hardly an exaggeration to deny that the permanence, productivity, and humanity of any industrial system depend upon its ability to utilize the positive and constructive impulses of all who work and upon its ability to arouse and continue interest in the necessary activities.
A. develop
B. efficiency
C. state
D. inspirational

34. The selection of managers on the basis of technical knowledge alone seems to recognize that the essential characteristic of management is getting things done through others, thereby demanding skills that are essential in coordinating the activities of subordinates.
A. training
B. fails
C. organization
D. improving

35. Only when it is deliberate and when it is clearly understood what impressions the ease of communication will probably create in the minds of employees and subordinate management, should top management refrain from commenting on a subject that is of general concern.
A. obvious
B. benefit
C. doubt
D. absence

36. Scientific planning of work requires careful analysis of facts and a precise plan of action for the whims and fancies of executives that often provide only a vague indication of the work to be done.
A. substitutes
B. development
C. preliminary
D. comprehensive

37. Within any single level of government, as a city or a state, the administrative authority may be concentrated or dispersed.
Of the following plans of government, the one in which administrative authority would be dispersed the MOST is the _____ plan.
    A. mayor
    B. mayor-council
    C. commission
    D. city manager

38. In general, the courts may review a decision of an administrative agency with rule-making powers. However, the courts will usually refuse to review a decision of such an agency if the only question raised concerning the decision is whether or not the
    A. decision contravenes public policy
    B. agency has abused the powers conferred upon it
    C. decision deals with an issue which is within the jurisdiction of the agency
    D. agency has applied the same rules of evidence as are used in the courts

39. A legislature sometimes delegates rule-making powers to the administrators of a public agency.
Of the following, the CHIEF advantage of such delegation is that
    A. the frequency with which the legality of the agency's rules is contested in court will be reduced
    B. the agency will have the flexibility to adjust to changing conditions and problems
    C. mistakes made by the administrators or the legislature in defining the scope of the agency's program may be easily corrected
    D. the legislature will not be required to approve the rules formulated by the agency

40. Some municipalities have delegated the functions of budget preparation and personnel selection to central agencies, thus removing these functions from operating departments.
Of the following, the MOST important reason by municipalities have delegated these functions to central agencies is that
    A. the performance of these functions presents problems that vary from one operating department to another
    B. operating departments often lack sufficient funds to perform these functions adequately
    C. the performance of these functions by a central agency produces more uniform policies than if these functions are performed by the operating departments
    D. central agencies are not controlled as closely as are operating departments and so have greater freedom in formulating new policies and procedures to deal with difficult budget and personnel problems

10 (#1)

41. Of the following, the MOST fundamental reason for the use of budgets in governmental administration is that budgets 41.____
    A. minimize seasonal variations in workloads and expenditures of public agencies
    B. facilitate decentralization of functions performed by public agencies
    C. provide advance control on the expenditure of funds
    D. establish valid bases for comparing present governmental activities with corresponding activities in previous periods

42. In some governmental jurisdictions, the chief executive prepares the budget for a fiscal period and presents it to the legislative branch of government for adoption. In other jurisdictions, the legislative branch prepares and adopts the budget. 42.____
    Preparation of the budget by the chief executive rather than by the legislative branch is
    A. *desirable*, primarily because the chief executive is held largely accountable by the public for the results of fiscal operations and should, therefore, be the one to prepare the budget
    B. *undesirable*, primarily because such a separation of the legislative and executive branches leads to the enactment of a budget that does not consider the overall needs of the government
    C. *desirable*, primarily because the preparation of the budget by the chief executive limits legislative review and evaluation of operating programs
    D. *undesirable*, primarily because responsibility for budget preparation should be placed in the branch that must eventually adopt the budget and appropriate the funds for it

43. The one of the following which is generally the FIRST step in the budget-making process of a municipality that has a central budget agency is 43.____
    A. determination of available sources of revenue within the municipality
    B. establishment of tax rates at levels sufficient to achieve a balanced budget in the following fiscal period
    C. evaluation by the central budget agency of the adequacy of the municipality's previous budgets
    D. assembling by the central budget agency of the proposed expenditures of each agency in the municipality for the following fiscal period

44. It is advantageous for a municipality to issue serial bonds rather than sinking fund bonds CHIEFLY because 44.____
    A. an issue of serial bonds usually includes a wider range of maturity dates than does an issue of sinking fund bond
    B. appropriations set aside periodically to retire serial bonds as they fall due are more readily invested in long-term securities at favorable rates of interest than are appropriations earmarked for redemption of sinking fund bonds
    C. serial bond are sold at regular intervals while sinking fund bonds are issued as the need for fund arises
    D. a greater variety of interest rates is usually offered in an issue of serial bonds than in an issue of sinking fund bond

45. Studies conducted by the Regional Plan Association of the 22-county New York Metropolitan Region, comprising New York City and surrounding counties in New York, New Jersey, and Connecticut, have defined Manhattan, Brooklyn, Queens, the Bronx, and Hudson County in New Jersey as the core. Such studies have examined the per capita personal income of the core as a percent of the per capita personal income of the entire Region, and the population of the core as a percent of the total population of the entire Region.
These studies support the conclusion that, as a percent of the entire Region,
   A. both population and per capita personal income in the core were higher in 2020 than in 1990
   B. both population and per capita personal income in the core were lower in 2020 than in 1990
   C. population was higher and per capita personal income was lower in the core in 2020 than in 1990
   D. population was lower and per capita personal income was higher in the core in 2020 than in 1990

45.____

KEY (CORRECT ANSWERS)

1. D	11. B	21. C	31. D	41. C
2. B	12. B	22. A	32. B	42. A
3. C	13. C	23. D	33. C	43. D
4. B	14. C	24. C	34. B	44. A
5. A	15. A	25. B	35. D	45. B
6. C	16. B	26. D	36. A	
7. B	17. C	27. C	37. C	
8. A	18. D	28. D	38. D	
9. D	19. B	29. A	39. B	
10. D	20. D	30. A	40. C	

SUPERVISION, ADMINISTRATION, MANAGEMENT, AND ORGANIZATION

EXAMINATION SECTION

TEST 1

DIRECTIONS: Each question or incomplete statement is followed by several suggested answers or completions. Select the one that BEST answers the question or completes the statement. *PRINT THE LETTER OF THE CORRECT ANSWER IN THE SPACE AT THE RIGHT.*

1. A supervisor scheduled and interview with a subordinate in order to discuss his unsatisfactory performance during the previous several weeks. The subordinate's work contained an excessive number of careless errors.
After the interview, the supervisor, reviewing his own approach for self-examination, listed three techniques he had used in the interview, as follows:
   I. Specifically pointed out to the subordinate where he had failed to meet the standards expected.
   II. Shared the blame for certain management errors that had irritated the subordinate.
   III. Agreed with the subordinate on specific targets to be met during the period ahead.
   Of the following statements, the one that is MOST acceptable concerning the above three techniques is that
   A. all 3 techniques are correct
   B. techniques I and II are correct; III is not correct
   C. techniques II and III are correct; I is not correct
   D. techniques I and III are correct; II is not correct

2. Assume that the performance of an employee is not satisfactory.
Of the following, the MOST effective way for a supervisor to attempt to improve the performance of the employee is to meet with him and to
   A. order him to change his behavior
   B. indicate the actions that are unsatisfactory and the penalties for them
   C. show him alternate ways of behaving and a method for him to evaluate his attempts at change
   D. suggest that he use the behavior of the supervisor as a model of acceptable conduct

3. Training employees to be productive workers is based on four fundamental principles:
   I. Demonstrate how the job should be done by telling and showing the correct operations step-by-step
   II. Allow the employee to get some of the feel of the job by allowing him to try it a bit
   III. Put him on the job while continuing to check his performance
   IV. Let him know why the job is important and why it must be done right

The MOST logical order for these training steps is:
A. I, III, II, IV   B. I, IV, II, III   C. II, I, III, IV   D. IV, I, II, III

4. Sometimes a supervisor is faced with the need to train under-educated new employees.
The following five statements relate to training such employees.
I. Make the training general rather than specific
II. Rely upon demonstrations and illustrations whenever possible
III. Overtrain rather than undertrain by erring on the side of imparting a little more skill than is absolutely necessary
IV. Provide lots of follow-up on the job
V. Reassure and recognize frequently in order to increase self-confidence
Which of the following choices lists all the above statements that are generally CORRECT?
A. I, II, IV   B. II, III, IV, V   C. I, II, V   D. I, II, IV, V

5. One of the ways in which some supervisors train subordinates is to discuss the subordinate's weaknesses with them. Experts who have explored the actual feelings and reactions of subordinates in such situations have come to the conclusion that such interviews USUALLY
A. are seen by subordinates as a threat to their self-esteem
B. give subordinates a feeling of importance which leads to better learning
C. convince subordinates to accept the opinion of the supervisor
D. result in the development of better supervision

6. The one of the following which BEST describes the rate at which a trainee learns departmental procedures is that he *probably* will learn
A. at the same rate throughout if the material to be learned is complex
B. slowly in the beginning and then learning will accelerate steadily
C. quickly for a while, than slow down temporarily
D. at the same rate if the material to be learned is lengthy

7. Which of the following statements concerning the delegation of work to subordinate employees is generally CORRECT?
A. A supervisor's personal attitude toward delegation has a minimal effect on his skill in delegating.
B. A willingness to let subordinates make mistakes has a place in work delegation.
C. The element of trust has little impact on the effectiveness of work delegation.
D. The establishment of controls does not enhance the process of delegation.

8. Assume that you are the chairman of a group that has been formed to discuss and solve a particular problem. After a half-hour of discussion, you feel that the group is wandering off the point and is no longer discussing the problem.
In this situation, it would be BEST for you to
A. wait to see whether the group will get back on the track by itself
B. ask the group to stop and to try a different approach

C. ask the group to stop, decide where they are going, and then to decide how to continue
D. ask the group to stop, decide where they are going, and then to continue in a different direction

9. One method of group decision-making is the use of committees. Following are four statements concerning committees.
   I. Considering the value of each individual member's time, committees are costly.
   II. One result of committee decisions is that no one may be held responsible for the decision.
   III. Committees will make decisions more promptly than individuals.
   IV. Committee decisions tend to be balanced and to take different viewpoints into account.
   Which of the following choices lists all of the above statements that are generally CORRECT?
   A. I and II B. II and III C. I, II, IV D. II, III, IV

10. Assume that an employee bypasses his supervisor and comes directly to you, the superior officer, to ask for a short leave of absence because of a pressing personal problem. The employee did not first consult with his immediate supervisor because he believes that his supervisor is unfavorably biased against him.
    Of the following, the MOST desirable way for you to handle this situation is to
    A. instruct the employee that is it not appropriate for him to go over the head of his supervisor regardless of their personal relationship
    B. listen to a brief description of his problem and then tactfully suggest that he take the matter up with his supervisor before coming to you
    C. request that both the employee and his supervisor meet jointly with you in order to discuss the employee's problem and to get at the reasons behind their apparent difficulty
    D. listen carefully to the employee's problem and then, without committing yourself one way or the other, promise to discuss it with his supervisor

11. Which of the following statements concerning the motivation of subordinates is generally INCORRECT? The
    A. authoritarian approach as the method of supervision is likely to result in the setting of minimal performance standards for themselves by subordinates
    B. encouragement of competition among subordinates may lead to deterioration of teamwork
    C. granting of benefits by a supervisor to subordinates in order to gain their gratitude will result in maximum output by the subordinates
    D. opportunity to achieve job satisfaction has an important effect on motivating subordinates

12. Of the following, the MOST serious disadvantage of having a supervisor evaluate subordinates on the basis of measurable performance goals that are set jointly by the supervisor and the subordinates is that this results-oriented appraisal method
    A. focuses on past performance rather than plans for the future
    B. fails to provide sufficient feedback to help subordinates learn where they stand
    C. encourages the subordinates to conceal poor performance and set low goals
    D. changes the primary task of the supervisor from helping subordinates improve to criticizing their performance

13. A supervisor can BEST provide on-the-job satisfaction for his subordinates by
    A. providing rewards for good performance
    B. allowing them to decide when to do the assigned work
    C. motivating them to perform according to accepted procedures
    D. providing challenging work that achieves departmental objectives

14. Which of the following factors generally contributes MOST to job satisfaction among supervisory employees?
    A. Autonomy and independence on the job
    B. Job security
    C. Pleasant physical working conditions
    D. Adequate economic rewards

15. Large bureaucracies typically exhibit certain characteristics.
    Of the following, it would be CORRECT to state that such bureaucracies generally
    A. tend to oversimplify communications
    B. pay undue attention to informal organizations
    C. develop an attitude of "group-think" and conformity
    D. emphasize personal growth among employees

16. When positive methods fail to achieve conformity with accepted standards of conduct or performance, a negative type of action, punitive in nature, usually must follow.
    The one of the following that is usually considered LEAST important for the success of such punishment or negative discipline is that it be
    A. certain   B. swift   C. severe   D. consistent

17. Assume that you are a supervisor. Philip Smith, who is under your supervision, informs you that James Jones, who is also your subordinate, has been creating antagonism and friction within the unit because of his unnecessarily gruff manner in dealing with his co-workers. Smith's remarks confirm your own observations of Jones' behavior and its effects.

In handling this situation, the one of the following procedures which will probably be MOST effective is to
- A. ask Smith to act as an informal counselor to Jones and report the results to you
- B. counsel the other employees in your unit on methods of changing attitudes of people
- C. interview Jones and help him to understand this problem
- D. order Jones to carry out his responsibilities with greater consideration for the feelings of his co-workers

18. The principle relating to the number of subordinates who can be supervised effectively by one supervisor is COMMONLY known as
    - A. span of control
    - B. delegation of authority
    - C. optimum personnel assignment
    - D. organizational factor

19. Ascertaining and improving the level of morale in a public agency is one of the responsibilities of a conscientious supervisor.
    The one of the following aspects of subordinates' behavior which is NOT an indication of low morale is
    - A. lower-level employees participating in organizational decision-making
    - B. careless treatment of equipment
    - C. general deterioration of personal appearance
    - D. formation of cliques

20. Employees may resist changes in agency operations even though such changes are often necessary. If you, as a supervisor, are attempting to introduce a necessary change, you should first fully explain the reasons for it to your staff.
    Your NEXT step should be to
    - A. set specific goals and outline programs for all employees
    - B. invite employee participation in effectuating the change by asking for suggestions to accomplish it
    - C. discuss the need for improved work performance by city employees
    - D. point out the penalties for non-cooperation without singling out any employee by name

21. A supervisor should normally void giving orders in an offhand or casual manner MAINLY because his subordinates
    - A. are like most people and may resent being treated lightly
    - B. may attach little importance to these orders
    - C. may work best if given the choice of work methods
    - D. are unlikely to need instructions in most matters

22. Assume that, as a supervisor, you have just praised a subordinate. While he expresses satisfaction at your praise, he complains that it does not help him get promoted even though he is on a promotion eligible list, since there is no current vacancy.

In these circumstances, it would be BEST for you to
- A. minimize the importance of advancement and emphasize the satisfaction in the work itself
- B. follow up by pointing out some errors he has committed in the past
- C. admit that the situation exists, and express the hope that it will improve
- D. tell him that, until quite recently, advancement was even slower

23. Departmental policies are usually broad rules or guides for action. It is important for a supervisor to understand his role with respect to policy implementation.
Of the following, the MOST accurate description of this role is that a supervisor should
    - A. be apologetic toward his subordinates when applying unpopular policies to them
    - B. act within policy limits, although he can attempt to influence policy change by making his thoughts and observations known to his superior
    - C. arrange his activities so that he is able to deal simultaneously with situations that involve several policy matters
    - D. refrain as much as possible from exercising permissible discretion in applying policy to matters under his control

23.____

24. A supervisor should be aware that most subordinates will ask questions at meetings or group discussions in order to
    - A. stimulate other employees to express their opinions
    - B. discover how they may be affected by the subjects under discussion
    - C. display their knowledge of the topics under discussion
    - D. consume time in order to avoid returning to their normal tasks

24.____

25. Don't assign responsibilities with conflicting objectives to the same work group. For example, to require a unit to monitor the quality of its own work is a bad practice.
This practice is MOST likely to be bad because
    - A. the chain of command will be unnecessarily lengthened
    - B. it is difficult to portray mixed duties accurately on an organization chart
    - C. employees may act in collusion to cover up poor work
    - D. the supervisor may delegate responsibilities which he should retain

25.____

KEY (CORRECT ANSWERS)

1. A
2. C
3. D
4. B
5. A

6. C
7. B
8. C
9. C
10. D

11. C
12. C
13. D
14. A
15. C

16. C
17. C
18. A
19. A
20. B

21. B
22. C
23. B
24. B
25. C

TEST 2

DIRECTIONS: Each question or incomplete statement is followed by several suggested answers or completions. Select the one that BEST answers the question or completes the statement. *PRINT THE LETTER OF THE CORRECT ANSWER IN THE SPACE AT THE RIGHT.*

1. Some supervisors use an approach in which each phase of the job is explained in broad terms supervision is general, and employees are allowed broad discretion in performing their job duties.
   Such a supervisory approach USUALLY affects employee motivation by
   A. improving morale and providing an incentive to work harder
   B. providing little or no incentive to work harder than the minimum required
   C. creating extra pressure, usually resulting in decreased performance
   D. reducing incentive to work and causing employees to feel neglected, particularly in performing complex tasks

1.____

2. An employee complains to a superior officer that he has been treated unfairly by his supervisor, stating that other employees have been given less work to do and shown other forms of favoritism.
   Of the following, the BEST thing for the superior officer to do FIRST in order to handle this problem is to
   A. try to discover whether the subordinate has a valid complaint or if something else is the real problem
   B. ask other employees whether they feel their treatment is consistent and fair
   C. ask his supervisor to explain the charges
   D. see that the number of cases assigned to this employee is reduced

2.____

3. Of the following, the MOST important condition needed to help a group of people to work well together and get the job done is
   A. higher salaries and a better working environment
   B. enough free time to relieve the tension
   C. good communication among everyone involved in the job
   D. assurance that everyone likes the work

3.____

4. A supervisor realizes that a subordinate has called in sick for three Mondays out of the past four. These absences have interfered with staff performance and have been part of the cause of the unit's "behind schedule" condition.
   In order to correct this situation, it would be BEST for the supervisor to
   A. order the subordinate to explain his abuse of sick leave
   B. discuss with the subordinate the penalties for abusing sick leave
   C. discuss the matter with his own supervisor
   D. ask the subordinate in private whether he has a problem about coming to work

4.____

2 (#2)

5. Of the following, the MOST effective way for a supervisor to minimize undesirable rumors about new policies in the units under his supervision is to
   A. bypass the supervisor and communicate directly with the individual members of the units
   B. supply immediate and accurate information to everyone who is supposed to be informed
   C. play down the importance of the rumors
   D. issue all communications in written form

6. Which of the following is an indication that a superior officer is delegating authority PROPERLY?
   A. The superior officer closely checks the work of experienced subordinates at all stages in order to maintain standards.
   B. The superior officer gives overlapping assignments to insure that work is completed on time.
   C. The work of his subordinates can proceed and be completed during the superior officer's absence.
   D. The work of each supervisor is reviewed by him more than once in order to insure quality.

7. Of the following supervisory practices, the one which is MOST likely to foster employee morale is for the supervisor to
   A. take an active interest in subordinates' personal lives
   B. ignore mistakes
   C. give praise when justified
   D. permit rules to go unenforced occasionally

8. As the supervisor who is responsible for the implementation of new paperwork procedure, you note that the workers often do not follow the stipulated procedure.
   Before taking action, it would be ADVISABLE to realize that
   A. unconscious behavior, such as failure to adapt to change, is largely uncontrollable
   B. new procedures sometimes have to be modified and adapted after being tried out
   C. threats of disciplinary action will encourage approval of change
   D. procedures that fail should be abandoned and replaced

9. The one of the following which is generally considered to be the MOST significant criticism of the modern practice of effective human relations in management of large organizations is that human relations
   A. weakens management authority over employees
   B. gives employees control of operations
   C. can be used to manipulate and control employees
   D. weakens unions

10. Of the following, the MOST important reason why the supervisor should promote good supervisor-subordinate relations is to encourage his staff to
    A. feel important
    B. be more receptive to control
    C. be happy in their work
    D. meet production performance levels

11. A superior officer decides to assign a special report directly to an employee, bypassing his supervisor.
    In general, this practice is
    A. *advisable*, chiefly because it broadens the superior officer's span of authority
    B. *inadvisable*, chiefly because it undermines the authority of the supervisor in the eyes of his subordinates
    C. *advisable*, chiefly because it reduces the number of details the supervisor must know
    D. *inadvisable*, chiefly because it gives too much work to the employee

12. Many supervisors make it a practice to solicit suggestions from their subordinates and to encourage their participation in decision-making.
    The success of this type of supervision usually depends MOST directly upon the
    A. quality of leadership provided by the supervisor
    B. number of the supervisor's immediate subordinates
    C. availability of opportunities for employee advancement
    D. degree to which work assignments cause problems

13. Small informal groups or "cliques" often appear in a work setting.
    The one of the following which is generally an advantage of such groups, from an administrative point of view, is that they
    A. are not influenced by the administrative set-up of the office
    B. encourage socializing after working hours
    C. develop leadership roles among the office staff
    D. provide a "steam valve" for release of tension and fatigue

14. Assume that you are a superior officer in charge of several supervisors who, in turn, are in charge of a number of employees. The employees who are supervised by Jones (a supervisor) come as a group to you and indicate several reasons why Jones is incompetent and "has to go."
    Of the following, your BEST course of action to take FIRST is to
    A. direct the employees to see Jones about the matter
    B. suggest to the employees that they should attempt to work with Jones until he can be transferred
    C. discuss the possibility of terminating Jones with your superior
    D. ask Jones about the comments of the employees after they depart

4 (#2)

15. Of the following, the MAIN effect which the delegation of authority can have on the efficiency of an organization is to
    A. reduce the risk of decision-making errors
    B. produce uniformity of policy and action
    C. facilitate speedier decisions and actions
    D. enable closer control of operations

16. Of the following, the main DISADVANTAGE of temporarily transferring a newly appointed worker to another unit because of an unexpected vacancy is that the temporary nature of his assignment will, MOST likely,
    A. undermine his incentive to orient himself to his new job
    B. interfere with his opportunities for future advancement
    C. result in friction between himself and his new co-workers
    D. place his new supervisor in a difficult and awkward position

17. Assume that you, as a supervisor, have decided to raise the quality of work produced by your subordinates.
    The BEST of the following procedures for you to follow is to
    A. develop mathematically precise standards
    B. appoint a committee of subordinates to set firm and exacting guidelines, including penalties for deviations
    C. modify standards developed by supervisors in other organizations
    D. provide consistent evaluation of subordinates' work, furnishing training whenever advisable

18. Assume that a supervisor under your supervision strongly objects whenever changes are proposed which would improve the efficiency of his unit.
    Of the following, the MOST desirable way for you to change his attitude is to
    A. involve him in the planning and formulation of changes
    B. promise to recommend him for a more challenging assignment if he accepts changes
    C. threaten to have him transferred to another unit if he does not accept changes
    D. ask him to go along with the changes on a tentative, trial basis

19. Work goals may be defined in terms of units produced or in terms of standards of performance.
    Which of the following statements concerning work goals is CORRECT?
    A. Workers who have a share in establishing goals tend to set a fairly high standard for themselves, but fail to work toward it.
    B. Workers tend to produce according to what they believe are the goals actually expected of them.
    C. Since workers usually produce less than the established goals, management should set goals higher than necessary.
    D. The individual differences of workers can be minimized by using strict goals and invariable procedures.

20. Of the following, the type of employee who would respond BEST to verbal instructions given in the form of a suggestion or wish is the
    A. experienced worker who is eager to please
    B. sensitive and emotional worker
    C. hostile worker who is somewhat lazy
    D. slow and methodical worker

21. As a supervisor, you note that the output of an experienced staff member has dropped dramatically during the last two months. In addition, his error rate is significantly above that of other staff members. When you ask the employee the reason for his poor performance, he says, "Well, it's rather personal and I would rather not talk about it if you don't mind."
    At this point, which of the following would be the BEST reply?
    A. Tell him that you will give him two weeks to improve or you will discuss the matter with your own supervisor
    B. Insist that he tell you the reason for his poor work and assure him that anything personal will be kept confidential
    C. Say that you don't want to interfere, but, at the same time, his work has deteriorated, and that you're concerned about it
    D. Explain in a friendly manner that you are going to place a warning letter in his personnel folder that states he has one month in which to improve

22. Research studies have shown that employees who are strongly interested in achievement and advancement on the job usually want assignments where the chance of success is _____, and desire _____ supervisory evaluation of their performance.
    A. low; frequent
    B. high; general
    C. high; infrequent
    D. moderate; specific

23. Of the following, a function of the supervisor that concerns itself with the process of determining a course of action from alternatives is USUALLY referred to as
    A. decentralization
    B. planning
    C. controlling
    D. input

24. Favorable working conditions are an important variable in producing an effective work unit.
    Which of the following would be LEAST conducive in providing a favorable work situation?
    A. Applying a job enrichment program to a routine clerical position
    B. Setting practical goals for the work unit which are consistent with the overall objective of the agency
    C. Assigning individuals to positions which require a higher level of educational achievement than that which they possess
    D. Establishing a communications system which distributes information and provides feedback to all organizational levels

25. Ever supervisor within an organization should know to whom he reports and who reports to him.
Within the organization, this will MOST likely insure
   A. unity of command
   B. confidentiality of sensitive issues
   C. excellent morale
   D. the elimination of the grapevine

25.____

KEY (CORRECT ANSWERS)

1. A
2. A
3. C
4. D
5. B

6. C
7. C
8. B
9. C
10. D

11. B
12. A
13. D
14. D
15. C

16. A
17. D
18. A
19. B
20. A

21. C
22. D
23. B
24. C
25. A

TEST 3

DIRECTIONS: Each question or incomplete statement is followed by several suggested answers or completions. Select the one that BEST answers the question or completes the statement. *PRINT THE LETTER OF THE CORRECT ANSWER IN THE SPACE AT THE RIGHT.*

1. In trying to improve the motivation of his subordinates, a supervisor can achieve the BEST results by taking action based upon the assumption that *most* employees
    A. have an inherent dislike of work
    B. wish to be closely directed
    C. are more interested in security than in assuming responsibility
    D. will exercise self-direction without coercion

2. Supervisors in public departments have many functions.
   Of the following, the function which is LEAST appropriate for a supervisor is to
    A. serve as a deputy for the administrator within his own unit
    B. determine needs within his unit and plan programs to meet these needs
    C. supervise, train, and evaluate all personnel assigned to his unit
    D. initiate and carry out fundraising projects, such as bazaars and carnivals, to buy needed equipment

3. When there are conflicts or tensions between top management and lower-level employees in any public department, the supervisor should FIRSTS attempt to
    A. represent and enforce the management point of view
    B. act as the representative of the workers to get their ideas across to management
    C. serve as a two-way spokesman, trying to interpret each side to the other
    D. remain neutral, but keep informed of changes in the situation

4. A probationary period for new employees is usually provided in public agencies.
   The MAJOR purpose of such a period is usually to
    A. allow a determination of employee's suitability for the position
    B. obtain evidence as to employee's ability to perform in a higher position
    C. conform to requirement that ethnic hiring goals be met for all positions
    D. train the new employee in the duties of the position

5. An effective program of orientation for new employees usually includes all of the following EXCEPT
    A. having the supervisor introduce the new employee to his job, outlining his responsibilities and how to carry them out
    B. permitting the new worker to tour the facility or department, so he can observe all parts of it in action
    C. scheduling meetings for new employees, at which the job requirements are explained to them and they are given personnel manuals
    D. testing the new worker on his skills, and sending him to a centralized in-service workshop

6. In-service training is an important responsibility of supervisors. 6.____
The MAJOR reason for such training is to
   A. avoid future grievance procedures, because employees might say they were not prepared to carry out their jobs
   B. maximize the effectiveness of the department by helping each employee perform at his full potential
   C. satisfy inspection teams from central headquarters of the department
   D. help prevent disagreements with members of the community

7. There are many forms of useful in-service training. 7.____
Of the following, the training method which is NOT an appropriate technique for leadership development is to
   A. provide special workshops or clinics in activity skills
   B. conduct pre-season institutes to familiarize new workers with the program of the department and with their roles
   C. schedule team meetings for problem-solving, including both supervisors and leaders
   D. have the leader rate himself on an evaluation form periodically

8. Of the following techniques of evaluating work training programs, the one that is BEST is to 8.____
   A. pass out a carefully designed questionnaire to the trainees at the completion of the program
   B. test the knowledge that trainees have both at the beginning of training and at its completion
   C. interview the trainees at the completion of the program
   D. evaluate performance before and after training for both a control group and an experimental group

9. Assume that a new supervisor is having difficulty making his instructions to subordinates clearly understood. 9.____
The one of the following which is the FIRST step he should take in dealing with this problem is to
   A. set up a training workshop in communication skills
   B. determine the extent and nature of the communication gap
   C. repeat both verbal and written instructions several times
   D. simplify his written and spoken vocabulary

10. Discipline of employees is usually a supervisor's responsibility. There may be several useful forms of disciplinary action in public employment. 10.____
Of the following, the form that is LEAST appropriate is the
   A. written reprimand or warning
   B. involuntary transfer to another work setting
   C. demotion or suspension
   D. assignment of added hours of work each week

3 (#3)

11. Of the following, the MOST effective means of dealing with employee disciplinary problems is to
    A. give personality tests to individuals to identify their psychological problems
    B. distribute and discuss a policy manual containing exact rules governing employee behavior
    C. establish a single, clear penalty to be imposed for all wrongdoing irrespective of degree
    D. have supervisors get to know employees well through social mingling

12. A recently developed technique for appraising work performance is to have the supervisor record on a continual basis all significant incidents in each subordinate's behavior that indicate unsuccessful action and those that indicate poor behavior.
    Of the following, a major DISADVANTAGE of this method of performance appraisal is that it
    A. often leads to overly close supervision
    B. results in competition among those subordinates being evaluated
    C. tends to result in superficial judgments
    D. lacks objectivity for evaluating performance

13. Assume that you are a supervisor and have observed the performance of an employee during a period of time. You have concluded that his performance needs improvement.
    In order to approve his performance, it would, therefore, be BEST for you to
    A. note your findings in the employee's personnel folder so that his behavior is a matter of record
    B. report the findings to the personnel officer so he can take prompt action
    C. schedule a problem-solving conference with the employee
    D. recommend his transfer to simpler duties

14. When an employee's absences or latenesses seem to be nearing excessiveness, the supervisor should speak with him to find out what the problem is.
    Of the following, if such a discussion produces no reasonable explanation, the discussion usually BEST serves to
    A. affirm clearly the supervisor's adherence to proper policy
    B. alert other employees that such behavior is unacceptable
    C. demonstrate that the supervisor truly represents higher management
    D. notify the employee that his behavior is being observed and evaluated

15. Assume that an employee willfully and recklessly violates an important agency regulation. The nature of the violation is of such magnitude that it demands immediate action, but the facts of the case are not entirely clear. Further assume that the supervisor is free to make any of the following recommendations.

The MOST appropriate action for the supervisor to take is to recommend that the employee be
A. discharged   B. suspended   C. forced to resign   D. transferred

16. Although employees' titles may be identical, each position in that title may be considerably different.
Of the following, a supervisor should carefully assign each employee to a specific position based PRIMARILY on the employee's
A. capability   B. experience   C. education   D. seniority

16.____

17. The one of the following situations where it is MOST appropriate to transfer an employee to a *similar* assignment is one in which the employee
    A. lacks motivation and interest
    B. experiences a personality conflict with his supervisor
    C. is negligent in the performance of his duties
    D. lacks capacity or ability to perform assigned tasks

17.____

18. The one of the following which is LEAST likely to be affected by improvement in the morale of personnel is employee
A. skill   B. absenteeism   C. turnover   D. job satisfaction

18.____

19. The one of the following situations in which it is LEAST appropriate for a supervisor to delegate authority to subordinates is where the supervisor
    A. lacks confidence in his own abilities to perform certain work
    B. is overburdened and cannot handle all his responsibilities
    C. refers all disciplinary problems to his subordinate
    D. has to deal with an emergency or crisis

19.____

20. Of the following, the BEST attitude toward the use of volunteers in programs is that volunteers should be
    A. discouraged, since they cannot be depended upon to show up regularly
    B. employed as a last resort when paid personnel are unavailable
    C. seen as an appropriate means of providing leadership, when effectively recruited and supervised
    D. eliminated to raise the professionalism of personnel

20.____

21. A supervisor finds that he is spending too much time on routine tasks, and not enough time on coordinating the work of his employees.
It would be MOST advisable for this supervisor to
    A. delegate the task of work coordination to a capable subordinate
    B. eliminate some of the routine tasks that the unit is required to perform
    C. assign some of the routine tasks to his subordinates
    D. postpone the performance of routine tasks until he has achieved proper coordination of his employees' work

21.____

22. Of the following, the MOST important reason for having an office manual in looseleaf form rather than in permanent binding is that the looseleaf form
    A. facilitates the addition of new material and the removal of obsolete material
    B. permits several people to use different sections of the manual at the same time
    C. is less expensive to prepare than permanent binding
    D. is more durable than permanent binding

23. In his first discussion with a newly appointed employee, the LEAST important of the following topics for a supervisor of a unit to include is the
    A. duties the subordinate is expected to perform on the job
    B. functions of the unit
    C. methods of determining standards of performance
    D. nature and duration of the training the subordinate will receive on the job

24. A supervisor has just been told by a subordinate, Mr. Jones, that another employee, Mr. Smith, deliberately disobeyed an important rule of the department by taking home some confidential departmental material.
    Of the following courses of action, it would be MOST advisable for the supervisor FIRST to
    A. discuss the matter privately, with both Mr. Jones and Mr. Smith at the same time
    B. call a meeting of the entire staff and discuss the matter generally without mentioning any employee by name
    C. arrange to supervise Mr. Smith's activities more closely
    D. discuss the matter privately with Mr. Smith

25. The one of the following actions which would be MOST efficient and economical for a supervisor to take to minimize the effect of seasonal fluctuations in the workload of his unit is to
    A. increase his permanent staff until it is large enough to handle the work of the busy season
    B. request the purchase of time and labor-saving equipment to be used primarily during the busy season
    C. lower, temporarily, the standards for quality of work performance during peak loads
    D. schedule for the slow season work that it is not essential to perform during the busy season

KEY (CORRECT ANSWERS)

1.	D	11.	B
2.	D	12.	A
3.	C	13.	C
4.	A	14.	D
5.	D	15.	B
6.	B	16.	A
7.	D	17.	B
8.	D	18.	A
9.	B	19.	C
10.	D	20.	C

21. C
22. A
23. C
24. D
25. D

TEST 4

DIRECTIONS: Each question or incomplete statement is followed by several suggested answers or completions. Select the one that BEST answers the question or completes the statement. *PRINT THE LETTER OF THE CORRECT ANSWER IN THE SPACE AT THE RIGHT.*

1. Assume that, while instructing a worker on a new procedure, the instructor asks, at frequent intervals, whether there are any questions.
   His asking for questions is a
   A. *good practice*, because it affords the worker an opportunity to participate actively in the lesson
   B. *good practice*, because it may reveal points that are not understood by the worker
   C. *poor practice*, because workers generally find it embarrassing to ask questions
   D. *poor practice*, because it may result in wasting time on irrelevant matters

2. Any person thoroughly familiar with the specific steps in a particular type of work is well-qualified to serve as a training course instructor in the work.
   This statement is *erroneous* CHIEFLY because
   A. a qualified instructor cannot be expected to have detailed information about many specific fields
   B. a person who knows a field thoroughly may not be good at passing his knowledge along to others
   C. it is practically impossible for any instructor to be acquainted with all the specific steps in a particular type of work
   D. what is true of one type of work is not necessarily true of other types of work

3. Of the following traits, the one that is LEAST essential for the "ideal" supervisor is that she
   A. be consistent in her interpretation of the rules and policies of the agency for which she works
   B. is able to judge a person's ability at her first meeting with that person
   C. know her own job thoroughly
   D. appreciate and acknowledge honest effort and above-average work

4. The one of the following which is generally the basic reason for using standard procedure is to
   A. serve as a basis for formulating policies
   B. provide the sequence of steps for handling recurring activities
   C. train new employees in the policies and objectives
   D. facilitate periodic review of standard practices

5. An employee, while working at the bookkeeping machine, accidentally kicks off the holdup alarm system. She notifies the supervisor that she can hear the holdup alarm bell ringing, and requests that the holdup alarm system be reset. After the holdup alarm system has been reset, the supervisor should notify the manager that the alarm
   A. is in proper working order
   B. should be shut off while the employee is working the bookkeeping machine to avoid another such accident
   C. kick-plate should be moved away from the worker's reception window so that it cannot be set off accidentally
   D. should be relocated so that it cannot be heard in the bookkeeping office

6. A supervisor who spends a considerate amount of time correcting subordinates' procedural errors should consider FIRST the possibility of
   A. disciplining those who make errors consistently
   B. instituting refresher training sessions
   C. redesigning work forms
   D. requesting that the requirements for entry-level jobs be changed

7. A supervisor has a subordinate who has been late the past four mornings. Of the following, the MOST important action for the supervisor to take FIRST is to
   A. read the rules concerning lateness to the employee in an authoritative manner
   B. give the subordinate a chance to explain the reason for his lateness
   C. tell the employee he must come in on time the next day
   D. ask the friends of the employee whether they can tell him the reason for the employee's lateness

8. During a conversation, a subordinate tells his supervisor about a family problem For the supervisor to give EXPLICIT advice to the subordinate would be
   A. *desirable*, primarily because a happy employee is more likely to be productive
   B. *undesirable*, primarily because the supervisor should not allow a subordinate to discuss personal problems
   C. *desirable*, primarily because their personal relations will show a marked improvement
   D. *undesirable*, primarily because a supervisor should not take responsibility for handling a subordinate's personal problem

9. As a supervisor, you have received instructions for a drastic change in the procedure for processing cases.
   Of the following, the approach which is MOST likely to result in acceptance of the change by your subordinates is for you to
   A. inform all subordinates of the change by written memo so that they will have guidelines to follow
   B. ask your superior to inform the unit members about the change at a staff meeting

C. recruit the most experienced employee in the unit to give individual instruction to the other unit members
D. discuss the change and the reasons for it with the staff so that they understand their role in its implementation

10. Of the following, the principle which should GENERALLY guide a supervisor in the training of employees under his supervision is that
    A. training of employees should be delegated to more experienced employees in the same title
    B. primary emphasis should be placed on training for future assignments
    C. the training process should be a highly individual matter
    D. training efforts should concentrate on employees who have the greatest potential

10._____

KEY (CORRECT ANSWERS)

1.	B		6.	B
2.	B		7.	B
3.	B		8.	D
4.	B		9.	D
5.	D		10.	C

INTERPRETING STATISTICAL DATA GRAPHS, CHARTS AND TABLES
TEST 1

DIRECTIONS: Each question or incomplete statement is followed by several suggested answers or completions. Select the one that BEST answers the question or completes the statement. *PRINT THE LETTER OF THE CORRECT ANSWER IN THE SPACE AT THE RIGHT.*

Questions 1-10.

DIRECTIONS: Questions 1 through 10 are to be answered SOLELY on the basis of the following table showing the amounts purchased by various purchasing units during 2018.

Purchasing Unit	First Quarter	Second Quarter	Third Quarter	Fourth Quarter
\multicolumn{5}{|c|}{DOLLAR VOLUME PURCHASED BY EACH PURCHASING UNIT DURING EACH QUARTER OF 2018 (FIGURES SHOWN REPRESENT THOUSANDS OF DOLLARS)}			
A	578	924	698	312
B	1,426	1,972	1,586	1,704
C	366	494	430	716
D	1,238	1,708	1,884	1,546
E	730	742	818	774
F	948	1,118	1,256	788

1. The total dollar value purchased by all of the purchasing units during 2018 approximated MOST NEARLY

   A. $2,000,000
   B. $4,000,000
   C. $20,000,000
   D. $40,000,000

   1___

2. During which quarter was the GREATEST total dollar amount of purchases made? _____ quarter.

   A. First   B. Second   C. Third   D. Fourth

   2___

3. Assume that the dollar volume purchased by Unit F during 2018 exceeded the dollar volume purchased by Unit F during 2017 by 50%
Then, the dollar volume purchased by Unit F during 2017 was

   A. $2,055,000
   B. $2,550,000
   C. $2,740,000
   D. $6,165,000

   3___

4. Which one of the following purchasing units showed the sharpest DECREASE in the amount purchased during the fourth quarter as compared with the third quarter? Unit

   A. A   B. B   C. D   D. E

   4___

91

5. Comparing the dollar volume purchased in the second quarter with the dollar volume purchased in the third quarter, the decrease in the dollar volume during the third quarter was PRIMARILY due to the decrease in the dollar volume purchased by Units _____ and _____.

   A. A; B   B. C; D   C. C; E   D. C; F

6. Of the following, the unit which had the LARGEST number of dollars of increased purchases from any one quarter to the next following quarter was Unit

   A. A   B. B   C. C   D. D

7. Of the following, the unit with the LARGEST dollar volume of purchases during the second half of 2018 was Unit

   A. A   B. B   C. D   D. F

8. Which one of the following MOST closely approximates the percentage which Unit B's total 2018 purchases represents of the total 2018 purchases of all units, including Unit B?

   A. 10%   B. 15%   C. 25%   D. 45%

9. Assume that research showed that each ten thousand dollars ($10,000) of purchases by Unit D during 2018 required an average of thirteen (13) man-hours of buyers' staff time. On that basis, which one of the following MOST closely approximates the number of man-hours of buyers' staff time required by Unit D during 2018?
   _____ man-hours.

   A. 1,800   B. 8,000   C. 68,000   D. 78,000

10. Assume that research showed that each ten thousand dollars ($10,000) of purchases by Unit C during 2018 required an average of ten (10) man-hours of buyers' staff time. This research also showed that during 2018 the average man-hours of buyers' staff time per ten thousand dollars of purchases required by Unit C exceeded by 25% the average man-hours of buyers' staff time per ten thousand dollars of purchases required by Unit E. On that basis, which one of the following MOST closely approximates the number of buyers' staff man-hours required by Unit E during 2018?
    _____ man-hours.

    A. 2,200   B. 2,400   C. 3,000   D. 3,700

KEY (CORRECT ANSWERS)

1. C   6. B
2. B   7. C
3. C   8. C
4. A   9. B
5. A   10. B

TEST 2

Questions 1-5.

DIRECTIONS: Questions 1 through 5 are to be answered SOLELY on the basis of the information below.

DEPARTMENT XYZ SIZE DISTRIBUTION OF PURCHASING ORDERS	
Amount of Order (dollars)	Number of Orders
1 - 9.99	91
10 - 19.99	135
20 - 49.99	320
50 - 99.99	712
100 - 199.99	1,050
200 - 499.99	735
500 - 999.99	305
1,000 - 1,999.99	94
2,000 - 4,999.99	36
5,000 - 9,999.99	18
10,000 - 19,999.99	3
20,000 - 49,000.99	1

1. The number of orders placed was
   A. 2600   B. 3500   C. 4000   D. 4500

2. Of the following graphs, most orders were between
   A. 50-200   B. 100-500   C. 200-2000   D. 10-100

3. The median value is approximately
   A. $100   B. $150   C. $200   D. $1050

4. Fewest orders were placed between
   A. $500-49,000.99   B. $10-49.99   C. $50-99.99   D. $200-499.99

5. The value of all the orders was more than
   A. $900,000
   B. $750,000
   C. $475,000
   D. one cannot tell from the information given

KEY (CORRECT ANSWERS)

1. B
2. B
3. B
4. B
5. C

TEST 3

Questions 1-4.

DIRECTIONS: Questions 1 through 4 are to be answered SOLELY on the basis of the information contained in the chart below.

COMPARATIVE WEIGHTS AND PRICES FOR 4 BRANDS OF PARMESAN CHEESE				
PRICES				
	SMALL	MEDIUM	LARGE	EXTRA LARGE
Brand W	1.16	$2.52	$5.20	$7.36
Brand X	.72	1.92	3.60	5.40
Brand Y	1.20	2.20	5.72	7.68
Brand Z	.60	1.16	3.36	6.24

WEIGHTS (IN OUNCES)				
	SMALL	MEDIUM	LARGE	EXTRA LARGE
Brand W	2	4 1/2	10	16
Brand X	1 1/2	4	9	15
Brand Y	2 1/2	5 1/2	11	16
Brand Z	1	2	6	12

1. Of the following, the brand and size of cheese which costs LEAST per ounce is Brand

   A. W, large
   B. X, extra large
   C. Y, medium
   D. Z, extra large

2. The brand which comes in a small size that costs the SAME per ounce as the extra large size is Brand

   A. W   B. X   C. Y   D. Z

3. Using a combination of the sizes listed in the above chart, the LEAST expensive price for exactly 1 pound, 11 ounces of Brand Z would be

   A. $12.52   B. $14.64   C. $14.80   D. $18.92

4. In the medium size, the brand that is LEAST expensive per ounce is Brand

   A. W   B. X   C. Y   D. Z

KEY (CORRECT ANSWERS)

1. B
2. C
3. B
4. C

TEST 4

Questions 1-4.

DIRECTIONS: Questions 1 through 4 are to be answered SOLELY on the basis of the following graph.

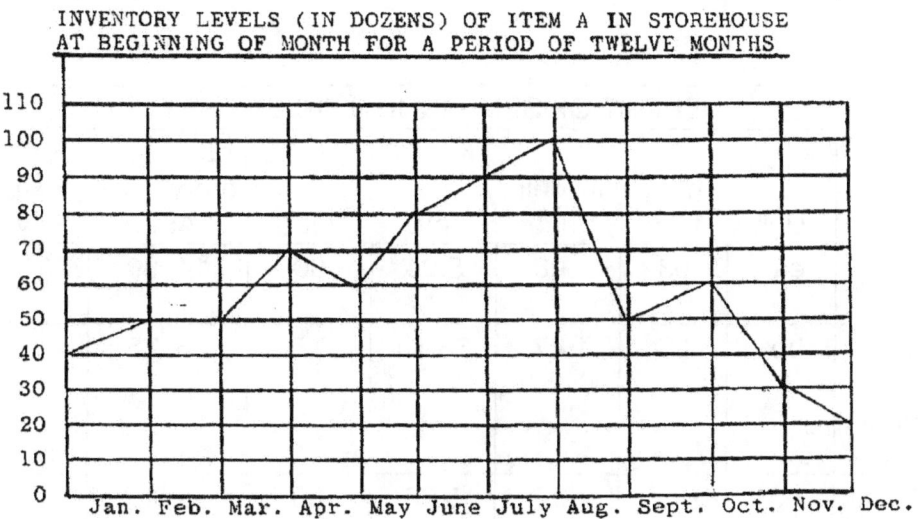

1. The average monthly inventory level during the course of the year was MOST NEARLY _____ dozen.

   A. 45   B. 60   C. 75   D. 90

2. If one dozen items fit in a carton measuring 2 feet by 2 feet by 3 feet, what MINIMUM volume would be required to store the maximum August inventory? _____ cubic feet.

   A. 12   B. 100   C. 700   D. 1,200

3. Assume that deliveries are made to the storehouse on the first working day of each month.
   If 30% of the June inventory was consumed during the month, how many items had to be delivered to reach the July inventory level? _____ items.

   A. 288   B. 408   C. 696   D. 1,080

4. Which three-month period contained the LOWEST average inventory level?

   A. Jan., Feb., March   B. April, May, June
   C. July, Aug., Sept.   D. Oct., Nov., Dec.

KEY (CORRECT ANSWERS)

1. B
2. D
3. B
4. D

TEST 5

Questions 1-6.

DIRECTIONS: Questions 1 through 6 are to be answered SOLELY on the basis of the following table.

REPORT OF SEMI-ANNUAL INVENTORY								
Article		Physical Inventory			Perpetual Inventory		Adjustment	
	Unit	Qty.	Price	Amt.	Qty.	Amt.	Qty.	Amt.
Batteries, flashlight	ea.	63	.08	5.04	60	14.80	+3	+.24
Bolts, flat head with square nuts, 100 in box	box	23	1.47	33.80	9,5	36.75		
Fuse, 15 amp, 4 in box	box	80	.07	5.60	80	5.60		
Fuse, 20 amp, 4 in box	box	77	.07	5.39	80	5.60	3	.21
Tape, friction, 50 ft. to a roll	roll	45	.22	9.90	45	9.90		
Washers, 100 in can 1/8" Beveled	can	35	.32	11.20	35	11.20		
3/8" Beveled	can	41	.33	13.63	45	14.85	4	1.32
Totals				84.47		88.70		

1. In the above report, for which item is there an INCORRECT entry?

    A. 15 amp fuses
    B. Friction tape
    C. Flashlight batteries
    D. 1/8" washers

2. In the above report, adjustments were omitted for _____ article(s).

    A. one B. two C. three D. four

3. After all appropriate entries have been made in the adjustment column, the total which must be deducted from the book value of the inventory is

    A. $1.53 B. $1.77 C. $4.23 D. $4.71

4. The quantities shown in Perpetual Inventory exceed those shown in Physical Inventory by a total of

    A. 4 B. 6 C. 10 D. 12

5. The cost of ten washers, 1/8" beveled, is MOST NEARLY 5____

    A. $.003   B. $.032   C. $.320   D. $3.20

6. The cost of 24 fuses is MOST NEARLY 6____

    A. $.28   B. $.42   C. $.80   D. $1.68

KEY (CORRECT ANSWERS)

1. C
2. A
3. C
4. B
5. B
6. B

TEST 6

Questions 1-10.

DIRECTIONS: Questions 1 through 10 are to be answered SOLELY on the basis of Tables I and II below.

TABLE I
Building 5 Storeroom
Report of Dollar Cost of Stores Issued to All Divisions in the Month Of December

Divisions	11 Dept. Reports & Bulletins	12 Food Supplies	13 Motor Vehicle Supplies	14 Office Supplies	15 Printed Stationery & Forms	16 Printing & Reproducing Supplies	17 Small Tools & Implements
A	40		125	85	13	55	45
B	21		231	35	46	32	61
C	68	422		75	37	81	
D	81			93	98	77	91
E	32	168		69	51	43	

TABLE II
Building 5 Storeroom
Summary of Dollar Cost of Stores Issued and Received and Balances, December

1 Supply Code	2 Balance Beginning of Month	3 Receipts from Vendors	4 Receipts from Storehouse A	5 Receipts from Storehouse B	6 Total Receipts	7 Total Issued	8 Balance
11	200	112	83	21	216	242	174
12	472	225	200	46	471	590	119
13	365	400			765	356	409
14	257	75	245	27	347	357	
15	245	89	152	36	277	255	277
16	281	104	190		294	288	287
17	197	32	110	40	182	197	182

1. The average value of small tools and implements received by Division C and E during the month of December

   A. is zero
   B. is approximately 78
   C. is 197
   D. cannot be determined from the information given

1___

2. The division which received the GREATEST dollar value of stores in the month of December was

   A. A B. B C. C D. D

   2____

3. The division which received the GREATEST number of items in all supply categories in December

   A. is A
   B. is B
   C. is D
   D. cannot be determined from the information given

   3____

4. In the column *Total Issued,* the entry which is INCORRECT is for

   A. Food Supplies
   B. Motor Vehicle Supplies
   C. Office Supplies
   D. Printed Stationery & Forms

   4____

5. In the column *Total Receipts,* the entry which is INCORRECT is for

   A. Department Reports & Bulletins
   B. Motor Vehicle Supplies
   C. Office Supplies
   D. Small Tools & Implements

   5____

6. The balance for Supply Code 14 has been omitted. This figure should be

   A. 10 B. 247 C. 367 D. 594

   6____

7. The balance has been INCORRECTLY entered for

   A. Department Reports & Bulletins
   B. Food Supplies
   C. Printing & Reproducing Supplies
   D. Small Tools & Implements

   7____

8. The dollar value of department reports and bulletins received from vendors in December exceeds that received from the storehouses by

   A. 8   B. 12
   C. 29   D. an indeterminate amount

   8____

9. For the classes of items received from Storehouse B during the month of December, the average dollar cost of these classes was MOST NEARLY

   A. 24 B. 34 C. 65 D. 170

   9____

10. One space is left blank in Column 4 of Table II.
    Judging only from the above tables, the MOST probable reason for this is that

    A. motor vehicle supplies were obtained from vendors only
    B. number 365 was inadvertently omitted from Column 4
    C. the figures for Columns 4 and 5 were included in Column 3
    D. the motor vehicle supply stock of Storehouse A is below the minimum stock level

    10____

KEY (CORRECT ANSWERS)

1. A
2. C
3. D
4. D
5. B

6. B
7. B
8. A
9. B
10. A

TEST 7

Questions 1-5.

DIRECTIONS: Questions 1 through 5 are to be answered SOLELY on the basis of the information given below.

CONTROLLED DRUG A					
Time Period	Purchase Order Number	Quantity Ordered	*Quantity Delivered By Vendor	Quantity Distributed During 2-wk Period	Inventory Balance at end of 2-wk Period
April 23-May 6	110,327	105 oz.	135 oz.	27 oz.	108 oz.
May 7 - May 20	111,437	42 oz.	40 oz.	39 oz.	109 oz.
May 21 - June 3	112,347	37 oz.	27 oz.	32 oz.	104 oz.
June 4 - June 17	112,473	35 oz.	35 oz.	45 oz.	94 oz.
June 18 - July 1	114,029	40 oz.	40 oz.	37 oz.	97 oz.

*Delivery is made on first day of time period.

1. The difference between Quantity Ordered and Quantity Delivered was GREATEST on Purchase Order Number

    A. 110,327   B. 111,437   C. 112,347   D. 112,473

2. The difference between the total number of ounces ordered and the total number of ounces delivered on April 23 through June 18 is _____ ounces.

    A. 17   B. 18   C. 19   D. 20

3. Suppose that average weekly usage was expected to be 26 ounces per week. Your supervisor has asked you to tell him whenever inventory balances get below a four-week level.
Under these conditions, you should have told your supervisor during the two-week period beginning

    A. April 23, May 21, June 4, June 18
    B. May 21, June 4, June 18
    C. May 21, June 18
    D. June 4, June 18

4. The GREATEST decreases in inventory balances happened between the two-week periods beginning

    A. April 23 and May 7   B. May 7 and May 21
    C. May 21 and June 4   D. June 4 and June 18

5. Suppose a new program has been started at your hospital and the weekly usage of Drug A is expected to be 52 ounces per week.
   If your supervisor must keep on hand a four-week supply, then the amount that should be delivered for the two-week period beginning on July 2 is _____ ounces.

   A. 52   B. III   C. 208   D. 211

KEY (CORRECT ANSWERS)

1. A
2. C
3. D
4. C
5. B

READING COMPREHENSION
UNDERSTANDING AND INTERPRETING WRITTEN MATERIAL
EXAMINATION SECTION
TEST 1

DIRECTIONS: Each question or incomplete statement is followed by several suggested answers or completions. Select the one that BEST answers the question or completes the statement. *PRINT THE LETTER OF THE CORRECT ANSWER IN THE SPACE AT THE RIGHT.*

Questions 1-10.

DIRECTIONS: Questions 1 through 10 are to be answered SOLELY on the basis of the DESCRIPTION OF ACCIDENT given below.

DESCRIPTION OF ACCIDENT

On Friday, May 9th, at about 2:30 P.M., Bus Operator Joe Able, Badge No. 1234, was operating his half-filled bus, Authority No. 5678, northbound along Fifth Ave. when a green Ford truck, N.Y. License No. 9012, driven by Sam Wood, came out of an Authority storeroom entrance into the path of the bus. To avoid hitting the truck, Joe Able turned his steering wheel sharply to the left, causing his bus to cross the solid white line into the opposite lane where the bus crashed head-on into a black 2015 Mercury, N.Y. License No. 3456, driven by Bill Green. The crash caused the Mercury to sideswipe a blue VW, N.J. License No. 7890, driven by Jim White, which was double-parked while he made a delivery. The sudden movement of the bus caused one of the passengers, Mrs. Jane Smith, to fall, striking her head on one of the seats. Joe Able blew his horn vigorously to summon aid, and Security Office Fred Norton, Badge No. 9876, and Stockman Al Blue, Badge No. 5432, came out of the storeroom and rendered assistance. While Norton gave Mrs. Smith first aid, Blue summoned an ambulance for Green. A tow truck removed Green's ca and Able found that the bus could operate under its own power, so he returned to the garage.

1. The Ford truck was driven by
   A. Able   B. Green   C. Wood   D. White

2. The Authority No. of the bus was
   A. 1234   B. 5678   C. 9012   D. 3456

3. The bus was driven by
   A. Able   B. Green   C. Wood   D. White

4. The license number of the VW was
   A. 9012   B. 3456   C. 7890   D. 5432

5. The horn of the bus summoned
   A. Blue   B. Green   C. White   D. Smith

6. The badge number of the security officer was
   A. 5432　　　B. 5678　　　C. 1234　　　D. 9876

7. The Mercury was driven by
   A. Smith　　　B. Norton　　　C. White　　　D. Green

8. The bus was traveling
   A. north　　　B. east　　　C. south　　　D. west

9. The vehicle towed away was a
   A. bus　　　B. Ford　　　C. Mercury　　　D. VW

10. Mrs. Smith hurt her
    A. head　　　B. back　　　C. arm　　　D. leg

Questions 11-12.

DIRECTIONS: Questions 11 and 12 are to be answered SOLELY on the basis of the following passage.

The City Charter requires that all purchases be made according to definite standards, or specifications. A specification may be defined as a statement of particulars descriptive of materials, or performance, or both; or, as a description of the technical details of a required commodity or service; or as a statement of what the buyer wants the seller to furnish. The specification should concisely define the quality of the commodity that is required to meet the needs of the using agency but still provide as wide competition in sources of supply as possible. To be of maximum value, the specification should describe the commodity clearly and in sufficient detail to ensure obtaining the exact commodity required.

11. Suppose that a buyer prepared the following specification for an item: cotton, absorbent, rolled.
    Based on the information given in the above passage, this specification would NOT be of value MAINLY because the
    A. quality of cotton requires is not described
    B. description is not concise
    C. mode of packaging is not stated
    D. using agency is not referred to

12. Based on the information given in the above passage, the MOST important indication that a specification has been well prepared is that the
    A. buyer gets few bids on the commodity
    B. commodity obtained meets the needs of the using agency
    C. commodity is procured at the lowest possible cost
    D. commodity is described in great detail.

Questions 13-15.

DIRECTIONS: Questions 13 through 15 are to be answered SOLELY on the basis of the following passage.

The receiving department should inspect the exterior condition of the packaging when a shipment is received before signing the dray ticket. When it is obvious that the package has been broken or dropped and there is apparent damage, this fact should be noted on such dray ticket. A clear receipt should not be given the carrier's representative unless the package, to all outward appearances, is undamaged. If the package is received in an undamaged condition and at a later date it is discovered that the material within the package is damaged, such concealed damage still gives the receiver an opportunity to make claim against the transportation company. However, a claim of concealed damage is more difficult to substantiate. When concealed damage is discovered, the carrier should be notified promptly of this fact by telephone, and a claim as well as a request for inspection should be made. Carriers usually insist that all packaging materials and cartons be retained by the receiving department until this inspection has been made by the carrier. Should the carrier decline the opportunity to inspect the damaged shipment, he merely informs the receiving department to go ahead and proceed with filing a claim. A claim number should be obtained when making such telephone call.

13. Of the following, the MOST suitable title for the foregoing passage is
    A. ACCEPTANCE OF MATERIAL UPON RECEIPT
    B. ESSENTIALS OF PROPER PACKAGING
    C. PROCEDURE FOR RETURNING DAMAGED MERCHANDISE
    D. THE IMPORTANCE OF THE DRAY TICKET IN SECURING COMPENSATION FOR DAMAGES

14. Of the following, the BEST evidence that the carrier had been notified of the existence of concealed damage would probably be the
    A. claim number
    B. defective merchandise
    C. dray ticket
    D. packaging materials if defective

15. Of the following, the MOST likely reason for the carrier's insistence that packaging materials be retained in the event of concealed damage until the carrier has made the inspection is that the carrier may
    A. be able to advise the supplier of the need to be more careful in the future in the selection of packaging materials
    B. be better able to train his employees in more efficient materials handling techniques
    C. have evidence in the event of an action by the carrier against the supplier
    D. utilize the same packaging materials in returning the defective merchandise to the supplier

Questions 16-18.

DIRECTIONS: Questions 16 through 18 are to be answered SOLELY on the basis of the following passage.

The use of a recognized brand name to describe a need is a method familiar to school purchasing officials. This is a simple tough not always satisfactory ordering description. It has the advantage of being more readily understood by the supplier, and the buyer can be assured of obtaining the desired manufacturer's product. The difficulty of attempting to express specific physical or chemical requirements is eliminated by accepting the manufacturer's formula. User acceptance may be more readily obtained because an established and familiar product is procured. A disadvantage of this method is that it eliminates competition at the manufacturer's level.

A purchasing agent often has the feeling that unless he makes complete use of purchase specifications, he is not doing an adequate buying job. Nothing is further from the truth. The other methods of describing quality are often used by the practicing purchasing agent. Not all requirements can be reduced to specific terms. Small purchases, of which schools have many, are not economically acquired by the use of purchase specifications because of the cost of preparing such specifications. It must also be remembered that when the purchaser does buy by specifications, he assumes responsibility for the performance of the product he specifies, since he has drawn the rules of how it is to be made and what its composition will be. Wise selection of the method of describing quality is perhaps a more essential prerequisite for a purchasing agent than the ability to prepare purchase specifications for each item he buys.

16. Of the following, the MOST suitable title for the foregoing passage would be 16.____
    A. ADVANTAGES OF BUYING BY SPECIFICATION
    B. BUYING IN SMALL QUANTITIES
    C. METHODS OF PURCHASING
    D. PREPARING THE PURCHASE SPECIFICATION

17. An advantage of buying by the use of a purchase specification implied by the author is that 17.____
    A. brand name merchandise is more likely to carry a warranty
    B. certain purchasing requirements cannot be expressed in writing with a high degree of precision
    C. it often enables purchasing in quantity at a lower cost based on specific needs
    D. purchase specifications can readily be prepared

18. According to the foregoing passage, an advantage of purchasing by brand name implied by the author is that 18.____
    A. brand name merchandise is nearly always more suited for long-term usage than unbranded merchandise
    B. it encourages bidding by manufacturers of like products
    C. manufacturers of brand name preparations change the formulas of their products
    D. persons generally prefer using a well-known item

Questions 19-24.

DIRECTIONS: Questions 19 through 24 are to be answered SOLELY on the basis of the following passage on THEFT.

THEFT

A security officer must be alert at all times to discourage the willful removal of property and material of the Authority by individuals for self-gain. Should a security officer detect such an individual, he should detain him and immediately call the supervisor at that location. No force should be used during the process of detainment. However, should the individual bolt from the premises, the security officer will be expected to offer some clues for his apprehension. Therefore, he should try to remember some characteristic traits about the individual, such as clothing, height, coloring, speech, and how he made his approach. Unusual characteristics, such as a scar or a limp, are most important. If a car is used, the security officer should take the license plate number of said car. Above information should be supplied to the responding peace officer and the special inspection control desk. In desolate locations, the security officer should first call the police and then the special inspection control desk. Any security officer having information of the theft should contact the director of special inspection by telephone or by mail. This information will be kept confidential if desired.

19. A security officer is required to be attentive on the job at all times MAINLY to
    A. get as much work done as possible
    B. prevent the stealing of Authority property
    C. show his supervisor that he is doing a good job
    D. prevent any other security officer from patrolling the area to which he is assigned

20. In the second sentence, the word *detain* means MOST NEARLY
    A. delay   B. avoid   C. call   D. report

21. The prescribed course of action a security officer should take when he discovers a person stealing Authority property is to
    A. make sure that all gates are closed to prevent the thief from escaping
    B. detain the thief and quickly call the supervisor
    C. use his club to keep the thief there until the police arrive
    D. call another security officer for assistance

22. The MOST useful of the following descriptions of a runaway thief would be that he is a
    A. tall man who runs fast
    B. man with blue eyes
    C. man with black hair
    D. tall man who limps

23. The license plate number of a car which is used by a thief to escape should be reported by a security officer to the responding peace officer and the
    A. director of protection agents
    B. security officer's supervisor
    C. special inspection control desk
    D. department of motor vehicles

24. A security officer patrolling a desolate area has spotted a thief. 24.____
    The security officer should FIRST call
    A. his supervisor
    B. the police
    C. the special inspection control desk
    D. the director of special inspection

Questions 25-30.

DIRECTIONS: Questions 1 through 10 are to be answered SOLELY on the basis of the following passage on REGISTRY SHEETS.

REGISTRY SHEETS

Where registry sheets are in effect, the security officer must legibly print Authority employee's pass number, title, license and vehicle number, destination, time in and time out; and each Authority employee must sign his or her name. The same procedure is to be applied to visitors, except in place of a pass number each visitor will indicate his address or firm name; and visitors must also sign waivers. Information is to be obtained from driver's license, firm credential card, or any other appropriate identification. All visitors must state their purpose for entering upon the property. If they desire to visit anyone, verification must be made before entry is permitted. All persons signing sheet must sign in when entering upon the property, and sign out again when leaving. The security officer will, at the end of his tour, draw a horizontal line across the entire sheet after his last entry, indicating the end of one tour and the beginning of another. At the top of each sheet, the security officer will enter the number of entries made during his tour, the sheet number, post, and date. Sheets are to begin with number 1 on the first day of the month and should be kept in numerical order. Each security officer will read the orders at each post to see whether any changes are made and at which hours control sheets are in effect.

25. Waivers need NOT be signed by 25.____
    A. Authority employees   B. vendors
    C. reporters   D. salesmen

26. All visitors are required to state 26.____
    A. whether they have a criminal record
    B. the reason for their visit
    C. the reason they are not bonded
    D. whether they have ever worked for the Authority

27. In the passage, the statement is made that *verification must be made before* 27.____
    entry is permitted.
    The word *verification* means MOST NEARLY
    A. allowance   B. confirmation   C. refusal   D. disposal

28. A security officer must draw a horizontal line across the entire registry sheet in order to show that 28.____
    A. he is being replaced to check a disturbance outside
    B. the last tour for the day has been completed
    C. one tour is ending and another is beginning
    D. a visitor has finished his business and is leaving

29. At the top of a registry sheet, it is NOT necessary for security officer to list the 29.____
    A. tour number   B. number of entries made
    C. sheet number   D. date

30. A security officer should check at which hours control sheets are in effect by reading 30.____
    A. registry sheet number 1 on the first day of each month
    B. the orders at each post
    C. the time in and time out that each person has entered on the registry sheet
    D. the last entry made on the registry sheet used before the start of his tour

KEY (CORRECT ANSWERS)

1.	C	11.	A	21.	B
2.	B	12.	B	22.	D
3.	A	13.	A	23.	C
4.	C	14.	A	24.	B
5.	A	15.	C	25.	A
6.	D	16.	C	26.	B
7.	D	17.	C	27.	B
8.	A	18.	D	28.	C
9.	C	19.	B	29.	A
10.	A	20.	A	30.	B

TEST 2

DIRECTIONS: Each question or incomplete statement is followed by several suggested answers or completions. Select the one that BEST answers the question or completes the statement. *PRINT THE LETTER OF THE CORRECT ANSWER IN THE SPACE AT THE RIGHT.*

Questions 1-4.

DIRECTIONS: Questions 1 through 4 are to be answered SOLELY on the basis of the following passage.

    The operation and maintenance of the stock-location system is a warehousing function and responsibility. The stock-location system shall consist of a file of stock-location record cards, either manually or mechanically prepared, depending upon the equipment available. The file shall contain an individual card for each stock item stored in the depot, with the records maintained in stock number sequence.

    The locator file is used for all receiving, warehousing, inventory, and shipping activities in he depot. The locator file must contain complete and accurate data to provide ready support to the various depot functions and activities, i.e., processing shipping documents, updating records on mechanized equipment, where applicable, supplying accurate locator information for stock selection and proper storage of receipts, consolidating storage locations of identical items not subject to shelf-life control, and preventing the consolidation of stock of limited shelf-life items. The file is also essential in accomplishing location surveys and the inventory program.

    Storage of bulk stock items by *spot location* method is generally recognized as the best means of obtaining maximum warehouse space utilization. Despite the fact that the spot-location method of storage enables full utilization of storage capacity, this method may prove inefficient unless it is supplemented by adequate stock-location control, including proper layout and accurate maintenance or stock-locator cards.

1. The manner in which the stock-location record cards should be filed is 1.____
   - A. alphabetically
   - B. chronological
   - C. numerically
   - D. randomly

2. Items of limited shelf-life should 2.____
   - A. not be stored
   - B. not be stored together
   - C. be stored in stock sequence
   - D. be stored together

3. Which one of the following is NOT mentioned in the passage as a use of the stock-location system? Aids in 3.____
   - A. accomplishing location surveys
   - B. providing information for stock selection
   - C. storing items received for the first time
   - D. processing shipping documents

110

4. If the spot-location method of storing is used, then the use of the stock-location system is
   A. *undesirable*, because the stock-location system is recognized as the best means of obtaining maximum warehouse space utilization
   B. *undesirable*, because additional records must be kept
   C. *desirable*, because stock-location controls are necessary with the spot-location storage method
   D. *undesirable*, because a stock-locator system will take up valuable storage space

Questions 5-8.

DIRECTIONS: Questions 5 through 8 are to be answered SOLELY on the basis of the following passage.

Known damage is defined as damage that is apparent and acknowledged by the carrier at the time of delivery to the purchaser. A meticulous inspection of the damaged goods should be completed by the purchaser, and a notation specifying the extent of the damage should be applied to the carrier's original freight bill. As is the case in known loss, it is necessary for the carrier's agent to acknowledge by signature the damage notation in order for it to have any legal status. The purchaser should not refuse damage freight since it is his legal duty to accept the property and to employ every available and reasonable means to protect the shipment and minimize the loss. Acceptance of a damaged shipment does not endanger any legitimate claim the purchaser may have against the carrier for damage. If the purchaser fails to observe the legal duty to accept damaged freight, the carrier may consider it abandoned. After properly notifying the vendor and purchaser of his intentions, the carrier may dispose of the material at public sale.

5. Before disposing of an abandoned shipment, the carrier MUST
   A. notify the vendor and the carrier's agent
   B. advise the vendor and purchaser of his plans
   C. notify the purchaser and the carrier's agent
   D. obtain the signature of the carrier's agent on the freight bill

6. In the case of damaged freight, the original freight bill will only have legal value if it is signed by the
   A. carrier's agent   B. purchaser
   C. vendor   D. purchaser and vendor

7. A purchaser does not protect a shipment of cargo that is damaged and is further deteriorating.
   According to the above passage, the action of the purchaser is
   A. *acceptable*, because he is not obligated to protect damaged cargo
   B. *unacceptable*, because damaged cargo must be protected no matter what is involved
   C. *acceptable*, because he took possession of the cargo
   D. *unacceptable*, because he is obligated by law to protect the cargo

8. The TWO requirements that must be satisfied before cargo can be labeled *known damage* are signs of evident damage and
   A. confirmation by the carrier or carrier's agent that this is so
   B. delayed shipment of goods
   C. signature of acceptance by the purchaser
   D. acknowledgment by the vendor that this is so

9. A hundred years ago, the steamboat was the center of life in the thriving Mississippi towns. Came the railroads; river traffic dwindled, and the white-painted vessels rotted at the wharves. During the World War, the government decided to relieve rail congestion by reviving the long-forgotten waterways. According to the above paragraph,
   A. the railroads were once the center of thriving river towns on the Mississippi River
   B. The volume of river transportation was greater than the volume of rail transportation during the World War
   C. business found river transportation more profitable than railroad transportation during the World War
   D. in the past century, the volume of transportation on the Mississippi River has varied

Questions 10-13.

DIRECTIONS: Questions 10 through 13 are to be answered SOLELY on the basis of the following paragraph.

Several special factors must be taken into account in selecting trucks to be used in a warehouse that stores food in freezer and cold storage rooms. Since gasoline fumes may contaminate the food, the trucks should be powered by electricity, not by gasoline. The trucks must be specially equipped to operate in the extreme cold of freezer rooms. The equipment must be dependable, for if a truck breaks down while transporting frozen food from a railroad car to the freezer or a warehouse, this expensive merchandise will quickly spoil. Finally, since cold storage and freezer rooms are expensive to operate, commodities must be stored close together, and the aisles between the rows of commodities must be as narrow as possible. Therefore, the trucks must be designed to work even in narrow aisles.

10. Of the following, the BEST title for the above passage is
    A. EXPENSES INVOLVED IN OPERATING A FREEZER OR COLD STORAGE ROOM
    B. HOW TO PREVENT FOOD SPOILAGE IN FREEZER AND COLD STORAGE ROOMS
    C. SELECTING THE BEST TRUCKS TO USE IN A FOOD STORAGE WAREHOUSE
    D. THE PROBLEM OF CONTAMINATION OF FOOD BY GASOLINE FUMES

4 (#2)

11. According to the above passage, electrically-powered trucks should be used for moving food in freezer and cold storage rooms CHIEFLY because they
    A. are cheaper to operate than gasoline-powered trucks
    B. are dependable
    C. can operate in extremes of heat and cold
    D. do not produce fumes which may contaminate food

11._____

12. Trucks designed for use in narrow aisles should be used in freezer and cold storage rooms because
    A. commodities are placed close together in freezer rooms to save space
    B. commodities spoil quickly if the space between aisles in the freezer is too wide
    C. narrow aisle trucks are more dependable
    D. narrow aisle trucks are run by electricity

12._____

13. According to the above passage, all of the following factors should be taken into account in selecting a truck for use to transport frozen food into and within a cold storage room EXCEPT
    A. ability to operate in extreme cold
    B. dependability
    C. the weight of the truck
    D. whether or not the truck emits exhaust fumes

13._____

Questions 14-18.

DIRECTIONS: Questions 14 through 18 are to be answered SOLELY on the basis of the information in the following passage.

Floors in warehouses, storerooms, and shipping rooms must be strong enough to stay level under heavy loads. Unevenness of floors may cause boxes of materials to topple and fall. Safe floor load capacities and maximum heights to which boxes may be stacked should be posted conspicuously so all can notice it. Where material in boxes, containers, or cartons of the same weight is regularly stored, it is good practice to paint a horizontal line on the wall indicating the maximum height to which the material may be piled. A qualified expert should determine floor load capacity from the building plans, the age and condition of the floor supports, the type of floor, and other related information.

Working aisles are those from which material is placed into and removed from storage. Working aisles are of two types: transportation aisles running the length of the building and cross aisles running across the width of the building. Deciding on the number, width, and location of working aisles is important. While aisles are necessary and determine boundaries of storage areas, they reduce the space actually used for storage.

14. According to the above passage, how should safe floor load capacities be made known to employees?
    They should be
    A. given out to each employee
    B. given to supervisors only
    C. printed in large red letters
    D. posted so that they are easily seen

14._____

113

15. According to the above passage, floor load capacities should be determined by
    A. warehouse supervisors
    B. the fire department
    C. qualified experts
    D. machine operators

16. According to the above passage, transportation aisles
    A. run the length of the building
    B. run across the width of the building
    C. are wider than cross aisles
    D. are shorter than cross aisles

17. According to the above passage, working aisles tend to
    A. take away space that could be used for storage
    B. add to space that could be used for storage
    C. slow down incoming stock
    D. speed up outgoing stock

18. According to the above passage, unevenness of floors may cause
    A. overall warehouse deterioration
    B. piles of stock to fall
    C. materials to spoil
    D. many worker injuries

Questions 19-22.

DIRECTIONS: Questions 19 through 22 are to be answered SOLELY on the basis of the information in the following passage.

Planning for the unloading of incoming trucks is not easy since generally little or no advance notice of truck arrivals is received. The height of the floor of truck bodies and loading platforms sometimes are different; this makes necessary the use of special unloading methods. When available, hydraulic ramps compensate for the differences in platform and truck floor levels. When hydraulic ramps are not available, forklift equipment can sometimes be used, if the truck springs are strong enough to support such equipment. In a situation like this, the unloading operation does not differ much from unloading railroad boxcar. In the cases where the forklift truck or a hydraulic pallet jack cannot be used inside the truck, a pallet dolly should be placed inside the truck, so that the empty pallet can be loaded close to the truck contents and rolled easily to the truck door and platform.

19. According to the above passage, unloading trucks is
    A. easy to plan since the time of arrival is usually known beforehand
    B. the same as loading a railroad boxcar
    C. hard to plan since trucks arrive without notice
    D. a very normal thing to do

20. According to the above passage, which materials handling equipment can make up for the difference in platform and truck floor levels?
    A. Hydraulic jacks
    B. Hydraulic ramps
    C. Forklift trucks
    D. Conveyors

21. According to the above passage, what materials handling equipment can be used when a truck cannot support the weight of forklift equipment?
    A. A pallet dolly
    B. A hydraulic ramp
    C. Bridge plates
    D. A warehouse tractor

22. Which is the BEST title for the above passage? 22._____
    A. UNLOADING RAILROAD BOXCARS
    B. UNLOADING MOTOR TRUCKS
    C. LOADING RAIL BOXCARS
    D. LOADING MOTOR TRUCKS

Questions 23-26.

DIRECTIONS: Questions 23 through 26 are to be answered SOLELY on the basis of the information in the following passage.

Planning for storage layout in terms of the supplies to be stored involves the intelligent and realistic application of a stockman's basic resources—space. The main objective of storage planning is the maximum use of available space. The planning and layout of space are dependent upon the types of supplies expected to be stored, and certain characteristics must be considered. Some supplies must be protected from dampness, extreme changes of temperature, and other such conditions. Iron and steel products rust quickly at high temperatures with high humidity. High temperatures also cause some plastics to melt and change shape, while extreme dampness can cause paper to mildew and wood to warp. Hazardous articles, including flammable items like paint and rubber cement, should be stored separately from each other and from other types of supplies.

Extremes in characteristics such as size, shape, and weight need to be considered in laying out space. Large, awkward containers and unusually heavy items generally should be stored near doors with aisles leading directly to them and/or shipping and receiving facilities. Light and fragile items cannot be stacked to a height which would cause crushing or other damage to containers and contents. Fast-moving articles should be stored in locations from which they can be handled quickly and efficient.

23. It is MOST important to store articles like paints and rubber cement in areas where 23._____
    A. they can be protected from theft
    B. shipping and receiving doors are easily accessible
    C. they can be isolated from other supplies
    D. boxes containing them can be stacked as high as possible

24. Storage locations from which items can be selected and issued quickly are recommended for supplies classified as 24._____
    A. fragile   B. fast-moving   C. under-sized   D. flammable

25. In order to prevent supplies made of iron from rusting, they should be stored in areas with _____ humidity and _____ temperature. 25._____
    A. low; high   B. low; low   C. high; high   D. high; low

26. Which of the following characteristics is NOT considered in the above passage on storage planning and layout? 26._____
    The _____ of the item to be stored.
    A. size   B. quantity   C. weight   D. shape

Questions 27-30.

DIRECTIONS: Questions 27 through 30 are to be answered SOLELY on the basis of the information in the following passage.

The *active stock* portion of the inventory is that portion which is kept for the purpose of satisfying the shop's expected requirements of that material. It is directly related to the *order quantity*. The *order quantity* is found by determining the expected annual requirements of the shop and dividing this by the number of orders for this merchandise which will be placed during the year. The most economical number of orders is usually found by considering the cost of ordering and storing inventory.

The *safety stock* portion of the inventory is that portion which is created to take care of above-average or unexpected demands on the inventory. This portion is directly related to the point at which the order is placed. The amount of safety stock is not determined by comparing order costs and carrying costs, but on the need for protection against stock shortages for each stock item under consideration. Some stock items will need more safety stock than others, depending upon how much the difference there has been in the past between the expected usage of material and the actual amount needed and used for any given time period, plus the reliability of the suppliers' delivery and of the order lead-time. If the expected usage of an item has always been 100% accurately predicted, then theoretically there would be no need for *safety stock*.

27. According to the above passage, the *active stock* inventory is that portion of the inventory which is
    A. used most frequently by management
    B. ordered on a regular basis, such as every month
    C. expected to meet the organization's anticipated inventory needs
    D. needed to protect against shortages in very active inventory items

28. According to the above passage, what factors must be considered to determine the order quantity for any active stock item?
    A. Anticipated requirements, ordering cost, and cost of storing inventory
    B. Order lead-time and delivery service
    C. Variety of stock items ordered in the previous year
    D. The largest quantity ever ordered

29. Maintaining a safety stock portion of the inventory is
    A. *good*, because it provides for unexpected demands on the inventory
    B. *good*, because it makes the inventory more valuable than it actually is
    C. *poor*, because it provides unnecessary work for stockmen since the inventory is rarely used
    D. *poor*, because it makes storage areas overcrowded and unsafe

30. The above passage indicates that 100 percent accuracy in forecasting future activity will eliminate the need for
    A. reliable deliveries
    B. active stock
    C. safety stock
    D. deviation in total order quantity

KEY (CORRECT ANSWERS)

1.	C	11.	D	21.	A
2.	B	12.	A	22.	B
3.	C	13.	C	23.	C
4.	C	14.	D	24.	B
5.	B	15.	C	25.	B
6.	A	16.	A	26.	B
7.	D	17.	A	27.	C
8.	A	18.	B	28.	A
9.	D	19.	C	29.	A
10.	C	20.	B	30.	C

PREPARING WRITTEN MATERIALS
EXAMINATION SECTION
TEST 1

DIRECTIONS: Each question or incomplete statement is followed by several suggested answers or completions. Select the one that BEST answers the question or completes the statement. *PRINT THE LETTER OF THE CORRECT ANSWER IN THE SPACE AT THE RIGHT.*

Questions 1-21.

DIRECTIONS: In each of the following sentences, which were taken from students' transcripts, there may be an error. Indicate the appropriate correction in the space at the right. If the sentence is correct as is, indicate this choice. Unnecessary changes will be considered incorrect.

1. In that building there seemed to be representatives of Teachers College, the Veterans Bureau, and the Businessmen's Association.
   A. Teacher's College
   B. Veterans' Bureau
   C. Businessmens Association
   D. Correct as is

   1.____

2. In his travels, he visited St. Paul, San Francisco, Springfield, Ohio, and Washington, D.C.
   A. Ohio and
   B. Saint Paul
   C. Washington, D.C.
   D. Correct as is

   2.____

3. As a result of their purchasing a controlling interest in the syndicate, it was well-known that the Bureau of Labor Statistics' calculations would be unimportant.
   A. of them purchasing
   B. well known
   C. Statistics
   D. Correct as is

   3.____

4. Walter Scott, Jr.'s, attempt to emulate his father's success was doomed to failure.
   A. Junior's,
   B. Scott's, Jr.
   C. Scott, Jr.'s attempt
   D. Correct as is

   4.____

5. About B.C. 250 the Romans invaded Great Britain, and remains of their highly developed civilization can still be seen.
   A. 250 B.C.
   B. Britain and
   C. highly-developed
   D. Correct as is

   5.____

6. The two boss's sons visited the children's department.
   A. bosses   B. bosses'   C. childrens'   D. Correct as is

   6.____

7. Miss Amex not only approved the report, but also decided that it needed no revision.
   A. report; but   B. report but   C. report. But   D. Correct as is

8. Here's brain food in a jiffy—economical, too!
   A. economical too!
   B. "brain food"
   C. jiffy-economical
   D. Correct as is

9. She said, "He likes the "Gatsby Look" very much."
   A. said "He
   B. "he
   C. 'Gatsby Look'
   D. Correct as is

10. We anticipate that we will be able to visit them briefly in Los Angeles on Wednesday after a five day visit.
    A. Wednes-   B. 5 day   C. five-day   D. Correct as is

11. She passed all her tests, and, she now has a good position.
    A. tests, and she
    B. past
    C. tests;
    D. Correct as is

12. The billing clerk said, "I will send the bill today"; however, that was a week ago, and it hasn't arrived yet!
    A. today;"   B. today,"   C. ago and   D. Correct as is

13. "She types at more-than-average speed," Miss Smith said, "but I feel that it is a result of marvelous concentration and self control on her part."
    A. more than average
    B. "But
    C. self-control
    D. Correct as is

14. The state of Alaska, the largest state in the union, is also the northernmost state.
    A. Union
    B. Northernmost State
    C. State of Alaska
    D. Correct as is

15. The memoirs of Ex-President Nixon, according to figures, sold more copies than <u>Six Crises</u>, the book he wrote in the '60s.
    A. Six Crises
    B. ex-President
    C. 60s
    D. Correct as is

16. "There are three principal elements, determining the hazard of buildings: the contents hazard, the fire resistance of the structure, and the character of the interior finish," concluded the speaker.
    The one of the following statements that is MOST acceptable is that, in the above passage,
    A. the comma following the word *elements* is incorrect
    B. the colon following the word *buildings* is incorrect
    C. the comma following the word *finish* is incorrect
    D. there is no error in the punctuation of the sentence

17. He spoke on his favorite topic, "Why We Will Win." (How could I stop him?)   17.____
    A. Win".   B. him?).   C. him)?   C. Correct as is

18. "All any insurance policy is, is a contract for services," said my insurance   18.____
    agent, Mr. Newton.
    A. Insurance Policy   B. Insurance Agent
    C. policy is is a   D. Correct as is

19. Inasmuch as the price list has now been up dated, we should sent it to the   19.____
    printer.
    A. In as much   B. updated
    C. pricelist   D. Correct as is

20. We feel that "Our know-how" is responsible for the improvement in technical   20.____
    developments.
    A. "our   B. know how   C. that,   D. Correct as is

21. Did Cortez conquer the Incas? the Aztecs? the South American Indians?   21.____
    A. Incas, the Aztecs, the South American Indians?
    B. Incas; the Aztecs; the South American Indians?
    C. south American Indians?
    D. Correct as is

22. Which one of the following forms for the typed name of the dictator in the closing   22.____
    lines of a letter is generally MOST acceptable in the United States?
    A. (Dr.) James F. Farley   B. Dr. James F. Farley
    C. Me. James J. Farley, Ph.D.   D. James F. Farley

23. The plural of   23.____
    A. turkey is turkies   B. cargo is cargoes
    C. bankruptcy is bankruptcys   D. son-in-law is son-in-laws

24. The abbreviation viz. means MOST NEARLY   24.____
    A. namely   B. for example
    C. the following   D. see

25. In the sentence, *A man in a light-gray suit waited thirty-five minutes in the*   25.____
    ante-room for the all-important document, the word IMPROPERLY hyphenated
    is
    A. light-gray   B. thirty-five   C. ante-room   D. all-important

KEY (CORRECT ANSWERS)

1.	D		11.	A
2.	C		12.	D
3.	B		13.	D
4.	D		14.	A
5.	A		15.	B
6.	B		16.	A
7.	B		17.	D
8.	D		18.	D
9.	C		19.	B
10.	C		20.	A

21. D
22. D
23. B
24. A
25. C

TEST 2

DIRECTIONS: Each question or incomplete statement is followed by several suggested answers or completions. Select the one that BEST answers the question or completes the statement. *PRINT THE LETTER OF THE CORRECT ANSWER IN THE SPACE AT THE RIGHT.*

Questions 1-10.

DIRECTIONS: In each of the following groups of four sentences, one sentence contains an error in sentence structure, grammar, usage, diction, or punctuation. Indicate the INCORRECT sentence.

1. A. The lecture finished, the audience began asking questions.
   B. Any man who could accomplish that task the world would regard as a hero.
   C. Our respect and admiration are mutual.
   D. George did like his mother told him, despite the importunities of his playmates.

2. A. I cannot but help admiring you for your dedication to your job.
   B. Because they had insisted upon showing us films of their travels, we have lost many friends whom we once cherished.
   C. I am constrained to admit that your remarks made me feel bad.
   D. My brother having been notified of his acceptance by the university of his choice, my father immediately made plans for a vacation.

3. A. In no other country is freedom of speech and assembly so jealously guarded.
   B. Being a beatnik, he felt that it would be a betrayal of his cause to wear shoes and socks at the same time.
   C. Riding over the Brooklyn Bridge gave us an opportunity to see the Manhattan skyline.
   D. In 1961, flaunting SEATO, the North Vietnamese crossed the line of demarcation.

4. A. I have enjoyed the study of the Spanish language not only because of its beauty and the opportunity it offers to understand the Hispanic culture but also to make use of it in the business associations I have in South America.
   B. The opinions he expressed were decidedly different from those he had held in his youth.
   C. Had he actually studied, he certainly would have passed.
   D. A supervisor should be patient, tactful, and firm.

5. A. At this point we were faced with only three alternatives: to push on, to remain where we were, or to return to the village.
   B. We had no choice but to forgive so venial a sin.
   C. In their new picture, the Warners are flouting tradition.
   D. Photographs taken revealed that 2.5 square miles had been burned.

6. A. He asked whether he might write to his friends.
    B. There are many problems which must be solved before we can be assured of world peace.
    C. Each person with whom I talked expressed his opinion freely.
    D. Holding on to my saddle with all my strength the horse galloped down the road at a terrifying pace.

7. A. After graduating high school, he obtained a position as a runner in Wall Street.
    B. Last night, in a radio address, the President urged us to subscribe to the Red Cross.
    C. In the evening, light spring rain cooled the streets.
    D. "Un-American" is a word which has been used even by those whose sympathies may well have been pro-Nazi.

8. A. It is hard to conceive of their not doing good work.
    B. Who won—you or I?
    C. He having read the speech caused much comment.
    D. Their finishing the work proves that it can be done.

9. A. Our course of study should not be different now than it was five years ago.
    B. I cannot deny myself the pleasure of publicly thanking the mayor for his actions.
    C. The article on "Morale" has appeared in the Times Literary Supplement.
    D. He died of tuberculosis contracted during service with the Allied Forces.

10. A. If it wasn't for a lucky accident, he would still be an office-clerk.
    B. It is evident that teachers need help.
    C. Rolls of postage stamps may be bought at stationery stores.
    D. Addressing machines are used by firms that publish magazines.

11. The one of the following sentences which contains NO error in usage is:
    A. After the robbers left, the proprietor stood tied in his chair for about two hours before help arrived.
    B. In the cellar I found the watchmans' hat and coat.
    C. The persons living in adjacent apartments stated that they had heard no unusual noises.
    D. Neither a knife or any firearms were found in the room.

12. The one of the following sentences which contains NO error in usage is:
    A. The policeman lay a firm hand on the suspect's shoulder.
    B. It is true that neither strength nor agility are the most important requirement for a good patrolman.
    C. Good citizens constantly strive to do more than merely comply the restraints imposed by society.
    D. Twenty years is considered a severe sentence for a felony.

13. Select the sentence containing an adverbial objective, 13.____
    A. Concepts can only acquire content when they are connected, however indirectly, with sensible experience.
    B. The cloth was several shades too light to match the skirt which she had discarded.
    C. The Gargantuan Hall of Commons became a tri-daily horror to Kurt, because two youths discerned that he had a beard and courageously told the world about it.
    D. Brooding morbidly over the event, Elsie found herself incapable of engaging in normal activity.

14. Select the sentence containing a verb in the subjunctive mood. 14.____
    A. Had he known of the new experiments with penicillin dust for the cure of colds, he might have been tempted to try them in his own office.
    B. I should be very much honored by your visit.
    C. Though he has one of the highest intelligence quotients in his group, he seems far below the average in actual achievement.
    D. Long had I known that he would be the man finally selected for such signal honors.

15. Select the sentence containing one (or more) passive perfect participle(s). 15.____
    A. Having been apprised of the consequences of his refusal to answer, the witness finally revealed the source of his information.
    B. To have been placed in such an uncomfortable position was perhaps unfair to a journalist of his reputation.
    C. When deprived of special immunity he had, of course, no alternative but to speak.
    D. Having been obdurate until now, he was reluctant to surrender under this final pressure exerted upon him.

16. Select the sentence containing a predicate nominative. 16.____
    A. His dying wish, which he expressed almost with his last breath, was to see that justice was done toward his estranged wife.
    B. So long as we continue to elect our officials in truly democratic fashion, we shall have the power to preserve our liberties.
    C. We could do nothing, at this juncture, but walk the five miles back to camp.
    D. There was the spaniel, wet and cold and miserable, waiting silently at the door.

17. Select the sentence containing exactly TWO adverbs. 17.____
    A. The gentlemen advanced with exasperating deliberateness, while his lonely partner waited.
    B. If you are well, will you come early?
    C. I think you have guessed right, though you were rather slow, I must say.
    D. The last hundred years have seen more change than a thousand years of the Roman Empire, than a hundred thousand years of the stone age.

Questions 18-24.

DIRECTIONS: Select the choice describing the error in the sentence.

18. If us seniors do not support school functions, who will? 18.____
    A. Unnecessary shift in tense   B. Incomplete sentence
    C. Improper case of pronoun   D. Lack of parallelism

19. The principal has issued regulations which, in my opinion, I think are too harsh. 19.____
    A. Incorrect punctuation   B. Faulty sentence structure
    C. Misspelling   D. Redundant expression

20. The freshmens' and sophomores' performances equaled those of the juniors and seniors. 20.____
    A. Ambiguous reference   B. Incorrect placement of punctuation
    C. Misspelling of past tense   D. Incomplete comparison

21. Each of them, Anne and her, is an outstanding pianist I can't tell you which one is best. 21.____
    A. Lack of agreement   B. Improper degree of comparison
    C. Incorrect case of pronoun   D. Run-on sentence

22. She wears clothes that are more expensive than my other friends. 22.____
    A. Misuse of *than*   B. Incorrect relative pronoun
    C. Shift in tense   D. Faulty comparison

23. At the very end of the story it implies that the children's father died tragically. 23.____
    A. Misuse of *implies*   B. Indefinite use of pronoun
    C. Incorrect spelling   D. Incorrect possessive

24. At the end of the game both of us, John and me, couldn't scarcely walk because we were so tired. 24.____
    A. Incorrect punctuation   B. Run-on sentence
    C. Incorrect case of pronoun   D. Double negative

Questions 25-30.

DIRECTIONS: Questions 25 through 30 consist of a sentence lacking certain needed punctuation. Pick as your answer the description of punctuation which will CORRECTLY complete the sentence.

25. If you take the time to keep up your daily correspondence you will no doubt be most efficient. 25.____
    A. Comma only after *doubt*
    B. Comma only after *correspondence*
    C. Commas after *correspondence*, *will*, and *be*
    D. Commas after *if*, *correspondence*, and *will*

26. Because he did not send the application soon enough he did not receive the up to date copy of the book.
    A. Commas after *application* and *enough*, and quotation marks before *up* and after *date*
    B. Commas after *application* and *enough*, and hyphens between *to* and *date*
    C. Comma after *enough*, and hyphens between *up* and *to* and between *to* and *date*
    D. Comma after *application*, and quotation marks before *up* and after *date*

27. The coordinator requested from the department the following items a letter each week summarizing progress personal forms and completed applications for tests.
    A. Commas after *items* and *completed*
    B. Semi-colon after *items* and *progress*, comma after *forms*
    C. Colon after *items*, commas after *progress* and *forms*
    D. Colon after *items*, commas after *forms* and *applications*

28. The supervisor asked Who will attend the conference next month.
    A. Comma after *asked*, period after *month*
    B. Period after *asked*, question mark after *month*
    C. Comma after *asked*, quotation marks before *Who*, quotation marks after *month*, and question mark after the quotation marks
    D. Comma after *asked*, quotation marks before *Who*, question mark after *month*, and quotation marks after the question mark

29. When the statistics are collected, we will forward the results to you as soon as possible.
    A. Comma after *you*
    B. Commas after *forward* and *you*
    C. Commas after *collected*, *results* and *you*
    D. Comma after *collected*

30. The ecology of our environment is concerned with mans pollution of the atmosphere.
    A. Comma after *ecology*
    B. Apostrophe after *n* and before *s* in *mans*
    C. Commas after *ecology* and *environment*
    D. Apostrophe after *s* in *mans*

KEY (CORRECT ANSWERS)

1.	D	11.	C	21.	B
2.	A	12.	D	22.	D
3.	D	13.	B	23.	B
4.	A	14.	A	24.	D
5.	B	15.	A	25.	B
6.	D	16.	A	26.	C
7.	A	17.	C	27.	C
8.	C	18.	C	28.	D
9.	A	19.	D	29.	D
10.	A	20.	B	30.	B

TEST 3

DIRECTIONS: Each question or incomplete statement is followed by several suggested answers or completions. Select the one that BEST answers the question or completes the statement. *PRINT THE LETTER OF THE CORRECT ANSWER IN THE SPACE AT THE RIGHT.*

Questions 1-6.

DIRECTIONS: From the four choices offered in Questions 1 through 6, select the one which is INCORRECT.

1.
   A. Before we try to extricate ourselves from this struggle in which we are now engaged in, we must be sure that we are not severing ties of honor and duty.
   B. Besides being an outstanding student, he is also a leader in school government and a trophy-winner in school sports.
   C. If the framers of the Constitution were to return to life for a day, their opinion of our amendments would be interesting.
   D. Since there are three m's in the word, it is frequently misspelled.

   1.____

2.
   A. It was a college with an excellance beyond question.
   B. The coach will accompany the winners, whomever they may be.
   C. The dean, together with some other faculty members, is planning a conference.
   D. The jury are arguing among themselves.

   2.____

3.
   A. This box is less nearly square than that one.
   B. Wagner is many persons' choice as the world's greatest composer.
   C. The habits of Copperheads are different from Diamond Backs.
   D. The teacher maintains that the child was insolent.

   3.____

4.
   A. There was a time when the Far North was unknown territory. Now American soldiers manning radar stations there wave to Boeing jet planes zooming by overhead.
   B. Exodus, the psalms, and Deuteronomy are all books of the Old Testament.
   C. Linda identified her china dishes by marking their bottoms with india ink.
   D. Harry S. Truman, former president of the United States, served as a captain in the American army during World War I.

   4.____

5.
   A. The sequel of their marriage was a divorce.
   B. We bought our car secondhand.
   C. His whereabouts is unknown.
   D. Jones offered to use his own car, providing the company would pay for gasoline, oil, and repairs,

   5.____

6. A. I read Golding's "Lord of the Flies".
   B. The orator at the civil rights rally thrilled the audience when he said, "I quote Robert Burns's line, 'A man's a man for a' that."
   C. The phrase "producer to consumer" is commonly used by market analysts.
   D. The lawyer shouted, "Is not this evidence illegal?"

Questions 7-9.

DIRECTIONS: In answering Questions 7 through 9, mark the letter A if faulty because of incorrect grammar, mark the letter B if faulty because of incorrect punctuation, mark the letter C if correct.

7. Mr. Brown our accountant, will audit the accounts next week.

8. Give the assignment to whomever is able to do it most efficiently.

9. The supervisor expected either your or I to file these reports.

Questions 10-14.

DIRECTIONS: In each of the following groups of four sentences, one sentence contains an error in sentence structure, grammar, usage, diction, or punctuation. Indicate the INCORRECT sentence.

10. A. The agent asked, "Did you say, 'Never again?'"
    B. Kindly let me know whether you can visit us on the 17th.
    C. "I cannot accept that!" he exploded. "Please show me something else.
    D. Ed, will you please lend me your grass shears for an hour or so.

11. A. Recalcitrant though he may have been, Alexander was willfully destructive.
    B. Everybody should look out for himself.
    C. John is one of those students who usually spends most of his time in the principal's office.
    D. She seems to feel that what is theirs is hers.

12. A. Be he ever so much in the wrong, I'll support the man while deploring his actions.
    B. The schools' lack of interest in consumer education is shortsighted.
    C. I think that Fitzgerald's finest stanza is one which includes the reference to youth's "sweet-scented manuscript.
    D. I never would agree to Anderson having full control of the company's policies.

13. A. We had to walk about five miles before finding a gas station.
    B. The willful sending of a false alarm has, and may, result in homicide.
    C. Please bring that book to me at once.
    D. Neither my sister nor I am interested in bowling.

14. A. He is one of the very few football players who doesn't wear a helmet with a face guard.
    B. But three volunteers appeared at the recruiting office.
    C. Such consideration as you can give us will be appreciated.
    D. When I left them, the group were disagreeing about the proposed legislation.

Question 15.

DIRECTIONS: Question 15 contains two sentences concerning criminal law. The sentences could contain errors in English grammar or usage. A sentence does not contain an error simply because it could be written in a different manner. In answering this question, choose answer
A. if only sentence I is correct
B. if only sentence II is correct
C. if both sentences are correct
D. if neither sentence is correct

15. I. The use of fire or explosives to destroy tangible property is proscribed by the criminal mischief provisions of the Revised Penal Law.
    II. The defendant's taking of a taxicab for the immediate purpose of affecting his escape did not constitute grand larceny.

KEY (CORRECT ANSWERS)

1.	A	6.	A	11.	C
2.	B	7.	B	12.	D
3.	C	8.	A	13.	B
4.	B	9.	A	14.	A
5.	D	10	A	15.	A

PREPARING WRITTEN MATERIAL

PARAGRAPH REARRANGEMENT
COMMENTARY

The sentences that follow are in scrambled order. You are to rearrange them in proper order and indicate the letter choice containing the correct answer at the space at the right.

Each group of sentences in this section is actually a paragraph presented in scrambled order. Each sentence in the group has a place in that paragraph; no sentence is to be left out. You are to read each group of sentences and decide upon the best order in which to put the sentences so as to form a well-organized paragraph.

The questions in this section measure the ability to solve a problem when all the facts relevant to its solution are not given.

More specifically, certain positions of responsibility and authority require the employee to discover connection between events sometimes, apparently, unrelated. In order to do this, the employee will find it necessary to correctly infer that unspecified events have probably occurred or are likely to occur. This ability becomes especially important when action must be taken on incomplete information.

Accordingly, these questions require competitors to choose among several suggested alternatives, each of which presents a different sequential arrangement of the events. Competitors must choose the MOST logical of the suggested sequences.

In order to do so, they may be required to draw on general knowledge to infer missing concepts or events that are essential to sequencing the given events. Competitors should be careful to infer only what is essential to the sequence. The plausibility of the wrong alternatives will always require the inclusion of unlikely events or of additional chains of events which are NOT essential to sequencing the given events.

It's very important to remember that you are looking for the best of the four possible choices, and that the best choice of all may not even be one of the answers you're given to choose from.

There is no one right way to solve these problems. Many people have found it helpful to first write out the order of the sentences, as they would have arranged them, on their scrap paper before looking at the possible answers. If their optimum answer is there, this can save them some time. If it isn't, this method can still give insight into solving the problem. Others find it most helpful to just go through each of the possible choices, contrasting each as they go along. You should use whatever method feels comfortable and works for you.

While most of these types of questions are not that difficult, we've added a higher percentage of the difficult type, just to give you more practice. Usually there are only one or two questions on this section that contain such subtle distinctions that you're unable to answer confidently. And you then may find yourself stuck deciding between two possible choices, neither of which you're sure about.

EXAMINATION SECTION
TEST 1

DIRECTIONS: The following groups of sentences need to be arranged in an order that makes sense. Select the letter preceding the sequence that represents the BEST sentence order. *PRINT THE LETTER OF THE CORRECT ANSWER IN THE SPACE AT THE RIGHT.*

1.
   I. The keyboard was purposely designed to be a little awkward to slow typists down.
   II. The arrangement of letters on the keyboard of a typewriter was not designed for the convenience of the typist.
   III. Fortunately, no one is suggesting that a new keyboard be designed right away.
   IV. If one were, we would have to learn to type all over again.
   V. The reason was that the early machines were slower than the typists and would jam easily.
   The CORRECT answer is:
   A. I, III, IV, II, V
   B. II, V, I, IV, III
   C. V, I, II, III, IV
   D. II, I, V, III, IV

1.____

2.
   I. The majority of the new service jobs are part-time or low-paying.
   II. According to the U.S. Bureau of Labor Statistics, jobs in the service sector constitute 72% of all jobs in this country.
   III. If more and more workers receive less and less money, who will buy the goods and services needed to keep the economy going?
   IV. The service sector is by far the fastest growing part of the United States economy.
   V. Some economists look upon this trend with great concern.
   The CORRECT answer is:
   A. II, IV, I, V, III
   B. II, III, IV, I, V
   C. V, IV, II, III, I
   D. III, I, II, IV, V

2.____

3.
   I. They can also affect one's endurance.
   II. This can stabilize blood sugar levels, and ensure that the brain is receiving a steady, constant, supply of glucose, so that one is *hitting on all cylinders* while taking the test.
   III. By food, we mean real food, not junk food or unhealthy snacks.
   IV. For this reason, it is important not to skip a meal, and to bring food with you to the exam.
   V. One's blood sugar levels can affect how clearly one is able to think and concentrate during an exam.
   The CORRECT answer is:
   A. V, IV, II, III, I
   B. V, II, I, IV, III
   C. V, I, IV, III, II
   D. V, IV, I, III, II

3.____

4. I. Those who are the embodiment of desire are absorbed in material quests, and those who are the embodiment of feeling are warriors who value power more than possession.
    II. These qualities are in everyone, but in different degrees.
    III. But those who value understanding yearn not for goods or victory, but for knowledge.
    IV. According to Plato, human behavior flows from three main sources: desire, emotion, and knowledge.
    V. In the perfect state, the industrial forces would produce but not rule, the military would protect but not rule, and the forces of knowledge, the philosopher kings, would reign.
    The CORRECT answer is:
    A. IV, V, I, II, III
    B. V, I, II, III, IV
    C. IV, III, II, I, V
    D. IV, II, I, III, V

5. I. Of the more than 26,000 tons of garbage produced daily in New York City, 12,000 tons arrive daily at Fresh Kills.
    II. In a month, enough garbage accumulates there to fill the Empire State Building.
    III. In 1937, the Supreme Court halted the practice of dumping the trash of New York City into the sea.
    IV. Although the garbage is compacted, in a few years the mounds of garbage at Fresh Kills will be the highest points south of Maine's Mount Desert Island on the Eastern Seaboard.
    V. Instead, tugboats now pull barges of much of the trash to Staten Island and the largest landfill in the world, Fresh Kills.
    The CORRECT answer is:
    A. III, V, IV, I, II
    B. III, V, II, IV, I
    C. III, V, I, II, IV
    D. III, II, V, IV, I

6. I. Communists rank equality very high, but freedom very low.
    II. Unlike communists, conservatives place a high value on freedom and a very low value on equality.
    III. A recent study demonstrated that one way to classify people's political beliefs is to look at the importance placed on two words: freedom and equality.
    IV. Thus, by demonstrating how members of these groups feel about the two words, the study has proved to be useful for political analysts in several European countries.
    V. According to the study, socialists and liberals rank both freedom and equality very high, while fascists rate both very low.
    The CORRECT answer is:
    A. III, V, I, II, IV
    B. V, IV, III, I, II
    C. III, V, IV, II, I
    D. III, I, II, IV, V

7. I. "Can there be anything more amazing than this?"
    II. If the riddle is successfully answered, his dead brothers will be brought back to life.
    III. "Even though man sees those around him dying every day," says Dharmaraj, "he still believes and acts as if he were immortal."
    IV. "What is the cause of ceaseless wonder?" asks the Lord of the Lake.
    V. In the ancient epic, The Mahabharata, a riddle is asked of one of the Pandava brothers.
    The CORRECT answer is:
    A. V, II, I, IV, III
    B. V, IV, III, I, II
    C. V, II, IV, III, I
    D. V, II, IV, I, III

8. I. On the contrary, the two main theories—the cooperative (neoclassical) theory and the radical (labor theory)—clearly rest on very different assumptions, which have very different ethical overtones.
    II. The distribution of income is the primary factor in determining the relative levels of material well-being that different groups or individuals attain.
    III. Of all issues in economics, the distribution of income is one of the most controversial.
    IV. The neoclassical theory tends to support the existing income distribution (or minor changes), while the labor theory ends to support substantial changes in the way income is distributed.
    V. The intensity of the controversy reflects the fact that different economic theories are not purely neutral, *detached* theories with no ethical or moral implications.
    The CORRECT answer is:
    A. II, I, V, IV, III
    B. III, II, V, I, IV
    C. III, V, II, I, IV
    D. III, V, IV, I, II

9. I. The pool acts as a broker and ensures that the cheapest power gets used first.
    II. Every six seconds, the pool's computer monitors all of the generating stations in the state and decides which to ask for more power and which to cut back.
    III. The buying and selling of electrical power is handled by the New York Power Pool in Guilderland, New York.
    IV. This is to the advantage of both the buying and selling utilities.
    V. The pool began operation in 1970, and consists of the state's eight electric utilities.
    The CORRECT answer is:
    A. V, I, II, III, IV
    B. IV, II, I, III, V
    C. III, V, I, IV, II
    D. V, III, IV, II, I

10.   I. Modern English is much simpler grammatically than Old English.
    II. Finnish grammar is very complicated; there are some fifteen cases, for example.
    III. Chinese, a very old language, may seem to be the exception, but it is the great number of characters/words that must be mastered that makes it so difficult to learn, not its grammar.
    IV. The newest literary language—that is, written as well as spoken—is Finish, whose literary roots go back only to about the middle of the nineteenth century.
    V. Contrary to popular belief, the longer a language is been in use the simpler its grammar—not the reverse.

The CORRECT answer is:
  A. IV, I, II, III, V
  B. V, I, IV, II, III
  C. I, II, IV, III, V
  D. IV, II, III, I, V

10.____

KEY (CORRECT ANSWERS)

1.	D	6.	A
2.	A	7.	C
3.	C	8.	B
4.	D	9.	C
5.	C	10.	B

TEST 2

DIRECTIONS: This type of question tests your ability to recognize accurate paraphrasing, well-constructed paragraphs, and appropriate style and tone. It is important that the answer you select contains only the facts or concepts given in the original sentences. It is also important that you be aware of incomplete sentences, inappropriate transitions, unsupported opinions, incorrect usage, and illogical sentence order. Paragraphs that do not include all the necessary facts and concepts, that distort them, or that add new ones are not considered correct.

The format for this section may vary. Sometimes, long paragraphs are given, and emphasis is placed on style and organization. Our first five questions are of this type. Other times, the paragraphs are shorter, and there is less emphasis on style and more emphasis on accurate representation of information. Our second group of five questions are of this nature.

For each of Questions 1 through 10, select the paragraph that BEST expresses the ideas contained in the sentences above it. *PRINT THE LETTER OF THE CORRECT ANSWER IN THE SPACE AT THE RIGHT.*

1. I. Listening skills are very important for managers.
    II. Listening skills are not usually emphasized.
    III. Whenever managers are depicted in books, manuals or the media, they are always talking, never listening.
    IV. We'd like you to read the enclosed handout on listening skills and to try to consciously apply them this week.
    V. We guarantee they will improve the quality of your interactions.

    A. Unfortunately, listening skills are not usually emphasized for managers. Managers are always depicted as talking, never listening. We'd like you to read the enclosed handout on listening skills. Please try to apply these principles this week. If you do, we guarantee they will improve the quality of your interactions.
    B. The enclosed handout on listening skills will be important improving the quality of your interactions. We guarantee it. All you have to do is take sometime this week to read and to consciously try to apply the principles. Listening skills are very important for manages, but they are not usually emphasized. Whenever managers are depicted in books, manuals or the media, they are always talking, never listening.
    C. Listening well is one of the most important skills a manager can have, yet it's not usually given much attention. Think about any representation of managers in books, manuals, or in the media that you may have seen. They're always talking, never listening. We'd like you to read the enclosed handout on listening skills and consciously try to apply them the rest of the week. We guarantee you will see a difference in the quality of your interactions.

1.____

D. Effective listening, one very important tool in the effective manager's arsenal, is usually not emphasized enough. The usual depiction of managers in books, manuals or the media is one in which they are always talking, never listening. We'd like you to read the enclosed handout and consciously try to apply the information contained therein throughout the rest of the week. We feel sure that you will see a marked difference in the quality of your interactions.

2.
I. Chekhov wrote three dramatic masterpieces which share certain themes and formats: Uncle Vanya, The Cherry Orchard, and The Three Sisters.
II. They are primarily concerned with the passage of time and how this erodes human aspirations.
III. The plays are haunted by the ghosts of the wasted life.
IV. The characters are concerned with life's lesser problems; however, such as the inability to make decisions, loyalty to the wrong cause, and the inability to be clear.
V. This results in sweet, almost aching, type of a sadness referred to as Chekhovian.

2.____

  A. Chekhov wrote three dramatic masterpieces: Uncle Vanya, The Cherry Orchard, and The Three Sisters. These masterpieces share certain themes and formats: the passage of time, how time erodes human aspirations, and the ghosts of wasted life. Each masterpiece is characterized by a sweet, almost aching, type of sadness that has become known as Chekhovian. The sweetness of this sadness hinges on the fact that it is not the great tragedies of life which are destroying these characters, but their minor flaws: indecisiveness, misplaced loyalty, unclarity.
  B. The Cherry Orchard, Uncle Vanya, and The Three Sisters are three dramatic masterpieces written by Chekhov that use similar formats to explore a common theme. Each is primarily concerned with the way that passing time wears down human aspirations, and each is haunted by the ghosts of the wasted life. The characters are shown struggling futilely with the lesser problems of life: indecisiveness, loyalty to the wrong cause, and the inability to be clear. These struggles create a mood of sweet, almost aching, sadness that has become known as Chekhovian.
  C. Chekhov's dramatic masterpieces are, along with The Cherry Orchard, Uncle Vanya, and The Three Sisters. These plays share certain thematic and formal similarities. They are concerned most of all with the passage of time and the way in which time erodes human aspirations. Each play is haunted by the specter of the wasted life. Chekhov's characters are caught, however, by life's lesser snares: indecisiveness, loyalty to the wrong cause, and unclarity. The characteristic mood is a sweet, almost aching type of sadness that has come to be known as Chekhovian.
  D. A Chekhovian mood is characterized by sweet, almost aching, sadness. The term comes from three dramatic tragedies by Chekhov which revolve around the sadness of a wasted life. The three masterpieces (Uncle Vanya, The Three Sisters, and The Cherry Orchard) share the same

theme and format. The plays are concerned with how the passage of time erodes human aspirations. They are peopled with characters who are struggling with life's lesser problems. These are people who are indecisive, loyal to the wrong causes, or are unable to make themselves clear.

3.
I. Movie previews have often helped producers decide which parts of movies they should take out or leave in.
II. The first 1933 preview of King Kong was very helpful to the producers because many people ran screaming from the theater and would not return when four men first attacked by Kong were eaten by giant spiders.
III. The 1950 premiere of Sunset Boulevard resulted in the filming of an entirely new beginning, and a delay of six months in the film's release.
IV. In the original opening scene, William Holden was in a morgue talking with thirty-six other "corpses" about the ways some of them had died.
V. When he began to tell them of his life with Gloria Swanson, the audience found this hilarious, instead of taking the scene seriously.

3.____

   A. Movie previews have often helped producers decide what parts of movies they should leave in or take out. For example, the first preview of King Kong in 1933 was very helpful. In one scene, four men were first attacked by Kong and then eaten by giant spiders. Many members of the audience ran screaming from the theater and would not return. The premiere of the 1950 film Sunset Boulevard was also very helpful. In the original opening scene, William Holden was in a morgue with thirty-six other "corpses," discussing the ways some of them had died. When he began to tell them of his life with Gloria Swanson, the audience found this hilarious. They were supposed to take the scene seriously. The result was a delay of six months in the release of the film while a new beginning was added.
   B. Movie previews have often helped producers decide whether they should change various parts of a movie. After the 1933 preview of King Kong, a scene in which four men who had been attacked by Kong were eaten by giant spiders was taken out as many people ran screaming from the theater and would not return. The 1950 premiere of Sunset Boulevard also led to some changes. In the original opening scene, William Holden was in a morgue talking with thirty-six other "corpses" about the ways some of them had died. When he began to tell them of his life with Gloria Swanson, the audience found this hilarious, instead of taking the scene seriously.
   C. What do Sunset Boulevard and King Kong have in common? Both show the value of using movie previews to test audience reaction. The first 1933 preview of King Kong showed that a scene showing four men being eaten by giant spiders after having been attacked by Kong was too frightening for many people. They ran screaming from the theater and couldn't be coaxed back. The 1950 premiere of Sunset Boulevard was also a scream, but not the kind the producers intended. The movie opens

with William Holden lying in a morgue discussing the ways they had died with thirty-six other "corpses." When he began to tell them of his life with Gloria Swanson, the audience couldn't take him seriously. Their laughter caused a six-month delay while the beginning was rewritten.

D. Producers very often use movie previews to decide if changes are needed. The premiere of Sunset Boulevard in 1950 led to a new beginning and a six-month delay in film release. At the beginning, William Holden and thirty-six other "corpses" discuss the ways some of them died. Rather than taking this seriously, the audience thought it was hilarious when he began to tell them of his life with Gloria Swanson. The first 1933 preview of King Kong was very helpful for its producers because one scene so terrified the audience that many of them ran screaming from the theater and would not return. In this particular scene, four men who had first been attacked by Kong were eaten by giant spiders.

4.
I. It is common for supervisors to view employees as "things" to be manipulated.
II. This approach does not motivate employees, nor does the carrot-and-stick approach because employees often recognize these behaviors and resent them.
III. Supervisors can change these behaviors by using self-inquiry and persistence.
IV. The best managers genuinely respect those they work with, are supportive and helpful, and are interested in working as a team with those they supervise.
V. They disagree with the Golden Rule that says "he or she who has the gold makes the rules."

4._____

A. Some managers act as if they think the Golden Rule means "he or she who has the gold makes the rules." They show disrespect to employees by seeing them as "things" to be manipulated. Obviously, this approach does not motivate employees any more than the carrot-and-stick approach motivates them. The employees are smart enough to spot these behaviors and resent them. On the other hand, the managers genuinely respect those they work with, are supportive and helpful, and are interested in working as a team. Self-inquiry and persistence can change even the former type of supervisor into the latter.
B. Many supervisors all into the trap of viewing employees as "things" to be manipulated, or try to motivate them by using a carrot-and-stick approach. These methods do not motivate employees, who often recognize the behaviors and resent them. Supervisors can change these behaviors, however, by using self-inquiry and persistence. The best managers are supportive and helpful, and have genuine respect for those with whom they work. They are interested in working as a team with those they supervise. To them, the Golden Rule is not "he or she who has the gold makes the rules."
C. Some supervisors see employees as "things" to be used or manipulated using a carrot-and-stick technique. These methods don't work. Employees often see through them and resent them. A supervisor who

wants to change may do so. The techniques of self-inquiry and persistence can be used to turn him or her into the type of supervisor who doesn't think the Golden Rule is "he or she who has the gold makes the rules." They may become like the best managers who treat those with whom they work with respect and give them help and support. These are the manager who know how to build a team.

    D. Unfortunately, many supervisors act as if their employees are objects whose movements they can position at will. This mistaken belief has the same result as another popular motivational technique—the carrot-and-stick approach. Both attitudes can lead to the same result—resentment from those employees who recognize the behaviors for what they are. Supervisors who recognize these behaviors can change through the use of persistence and the use of self-inquiry. It's important to remember that the best managers respect their employees. They readily give necessary help and support and are interested in working as a team with those they supervise. To these managers, the Golden Rule is not "he or she who has the gold makes the rules."

5.
  I. The first half of the nineteenth century produced a group of pessimistic poets—Byron, De Musset, Heine, Pushkin, and Leopardi.
  II. It also produced a group of pessimistic composers—Schubert, Chopin, Schumann, and even the later Beethoven.
 III. Above all, in philosophy, there was the profoundly pessimistic philosopher, Schopenhauer.
 IV. The Revolution was dead, the Bourbons were restored, the feudal barons were reclaiming their land, and progress everywhere was being suppressed, as the great age was over.
  V. "I thank God," said Goethe, "that I am not young in so thoroughly finished a world."

    A. "I thank God," said Goethe, "that I am not young in so thoroughly finished a world." The Revolution was dead, the Bourbons were restored, the feudal barons were reclaiming their land, and progress everywhere was being suppressed. The first half of the nineteenth century produced a group of pessimistic poets: Byron, De Musset, Heine, Pushkin, and Leopardi. It also produced pessimistic composers: Schubert, Chopin, Schumann. Although Beethoven came later, he fits into this group, too. Finally and above all, it also produced a profoundly pessimistic philosopher, Schopenhauer. The great age was over.
    B. The first half of the nineteenth century produced a group of pessimistic poets: Byron, De Musset, Heine, Pushkin, and Leopardi. It produced a group of pessimistic composers: Schubert, Chopin, Schumann, and even the later Beethoven. Above all, it produced a profoundly pessimistic philosopher, Schopenhauer. For each of these men, the great age was over. The Revolution was dead, and the Bourbons were restored. The feudal barons were reclaiming their land, and progress everywhere was being suppressed.

C. The great age was over. The Revolution was dead—the Bourbons were restored, and the feudal barons were reclaiming their land. Progress everywhere was being suppressed. Out of this climate came a profound pessimism. Poets, like Byron, De Musset, Heine, Pushkin, and Leopardi; composers, like Schubert, Chopin, Schumann, and even the later Beethoven; and above all, a profoundly pessimistic philosopher, Schopenauer. This pessimism which arose in the first half of the nineteenth century is illustrated by these words of Goethe, "I thank God that I am not young in so thoroughly finished a world."
D. The first half of the nineteenth century produced a group of pessimistic poets, Byron, De Musset, Heine, Pushkin, and Leopardi—and a group of pessimistic composers, Schubert, Chopin, Schumann, and the later Beethoven. Above it all, it produced a profoundly pessimistic philosopher, Schopenhauer. The great age was over. The Revolution was dead, the Bourbons were restored, the feudal barons were reclaiming their land, and progress everywhere was being suppressed. "I thank God," said Goethe, "that I am not young in so thoroughly finished a world."

6.   I. A new manager sometimes may feel insecure about his or her competence in the new position.
    II. The new manager may then exhibit defensive or arrogant behavior towards those one supervises, or the new manager may direct overly flattering behavior toward one's new supervisor.

6.____

    A. Sometimes, a new manager may feel insecure about his or her ability to perform well in this new position. The insecurity may lead him or her to treat others differently. He or she may display arrogant or defensive behavior towards those he or she supervises, or be overly flattering to his or her new supervisor.
    B. A new manager may sometimes feel insecure about his or her ability to perform well in the new position. He or she may then become arrogant, defensive, or overly flattering towards those he or she works with.
    C. There are times when a new manager may be insecure about how well he or she can perform in the new job. The new manager may also behave defensive or act in an arrogant way towards those he or she supervises, or overly flatter his or her boss.
    D. Sometimes a new manager may feel insecure about his or her ability to perform well in the new position. He or she may then display arrogant or defensive behavior towards those they supervise, or become overly flattering towards their supervisors.

7.   I. It is possible to eliminate unwanted behavior by bringing it under stimulus control—tying the behavior to a cue, and then never, or rarely, giving the cue.
    II. One trainer successfully used this method to keep an energetic young porpoise from coming out of her tank whenever she felt like it, which was potentially dangerous.
    III. Her trainer taught her to do it for a reward, in response to a hand signal, and then rarely gave the signal.

7.____

A. Unwanted behavior can be eliminated by tying the behavior to a cue, and then never, or rarely, giving the cue. This is called stimulus control. One trainer was able to use this method to keep an energetic young porpoise from coming out of her tank by teaching her to come out for a reward in response to a hand signal, and then rarely giving the signal.

B. Stimulus control can be used to eliminate unwanted behavior. In this method, behavior is tied to a cue, and then the cue is rarely, if ever, given. One trainer was able to successfully use stimulus control to keep an energetic young porpoise from coming out of her tank whenever she felt like it—a potentially dangerous practice. She taught the porpoise to come out for a reward when she gave a hand signal, and then rarely gave the signal.

C. It is possible to eliminate behavior that is undesirable by bringing it under stimulus control by tying behavior to a signal, and then rarely giving the signal. One trainer successfully used this method to keep an energetic porpoise from coming out of her tank, a potentially dangerous situation. Her trainer taught the porpoise to do it for a reward, in response to a hand signal, and then would rarely give the signal.

D. By using stimulus control, it is possible to eliminate unwanted behavior by tying the behavior to a cue, and then rarely or never give the cue. One trainer was able to use this method to successfully stop a young porpoise from coming out of her tank whenever she felt like it. To curb this potentially dangerous practice, the porpoise was taught by the trainer to come out of the tank for a reward, in response to a hand signal, and then rarely given the signal.

8.
I. There is a great deal of concern over the safety of commercial trucks, caused by their greatly increased role in serious accidents since federal deregulation in 1981.
II. Recently, 60 percent of trucks in New York and Connecticut and 70 percent of trucks in Maryland randomly stopped by state troopers failed safety inspections.
III. Sixteen states in the United States require no training at all for truck drivers.

8.____

A. Since federal deregulation in 1981, there has been a great deal of concern over the safety of commercial trucks, and their greatly increased role in serious accidents. Recently, 60 percent of trucks in New York and Connecticut, and 70 percent of trucks in Maryland failed safety inspections. Sixteen states in the United States require no training at all for truck drivers.

B. There is a great deal of concern over the safety of commercial trucks since federal deregulation in 1981. Their role in serious accidents has greatly increased. Recently, 60 percent of trucks randomly stopped in Connecticut and New York and 70 percent in Maryland failed safety inspections conducted by state troopers. Sixteen states in the United States provide no training at all for truck drivers.

C. Commercial trucks have a greatly increased role in serious accidents since federal deregulation in 1981. This has led to a great deal of concern.

Recently, 70 percent of trucks in Maryland and 60 percent of trucks in New York and Connecticut failed inspection of those that were randomly stopped by state troopers. Sixteen states in the United States require no training for all truck drivers.

D. Since federal deregulation in 1981, the role that commercial trucks have played in serious accidents has greatly increased, and this has led to a great deal of concern. Recently, 60 percent of trucks in New York and Connecticut, and 70 percent of trucks in Maryland randomly stopped by state troopers failed safety inspections. Sixteen states in the U.S. don't require any training for truck drivers.

9.
I. No matter how much some people have, they still feel unsatisfied and want more, or want to keep what they have forever.
II. One recent television documentary showed several people flying from New York to Paris for a one-day shopping spree to buy platinum earrings, because they were bored.
III. In Brazil, some people were ordering coffins that cost a minimum of $45,000 and are equipping them with deluxe stereos, televisions, and other graveyard necessities.

9.____

A. Some people, despite having a great deal, still feel unsatisfied and want more, or think they can keep what they have forever. One recent documentary on television showed several people enroute from Paris to New York for a one day shopping spree to buy platinum earrings, because they were bored. Some people in Brazil are even ordering coffins equipped with such graveyard necessities as deluxe stereos and televisions. The price of the coffins start at $45,000.
B. No matter how much some people have, they may feel unsatisfied. This leads them to want more, or to want to keep what they have forever. Recently, a television documentary depicting several people flying from New York to Paris for a one day shopping spree to buy platinum earrings. They were bored. Some people in Brazil are ordering coffins that cost at least $45,000 and come equipped with deluxe televisions, stereos and other necessary graveyard items.
C. Some people will be dissatisfied no matter how much they have. They may want more, or they may want to keep what they have forever. One recent television documentary showed several people, motivated by boredom, jetting from New York to Paris for a one-day shopping spree to buy platinum earrings. In Brazil, some people are ordering coffins equipped with deluxe stereos, televisions and other graveyard necessities. The minimum price for these coffins—$45,000.
D. Some people are never satisfied. No matter how much they have they still want more, or think they can keep what they have forever. One television documentary recently showed several people flying from New York to Paris for the day to buy platinum earrings because they were bored. In Brazil, some people are ordering coffins that cost $45,000 and are equipped with deluxe stereos, televisions and other graveyard necessities.

10. I. A television signal or video signal has three parts.
    II. Its parts are the black-and-white portion, the color portion, and the synchronizing (sync) pulses, which keep the picture stable.
    III. Each video source, whether it's a camera or a video-cassette recorder contains its own generator of these synchronizing pulses to accompany the picture that it's sending in order to keep it steady and straight.
    IV. In order to produce a clean recording, a video-cassette recorder must "lock-up" to the sync pulses that are part of the video it is trying to record, and this effort may be very noticeable if the device does not have gunlock.

    A. There are three parts to a television or video signal: the black-and-white part, the color part, and the synchronizing (sync) pulses, which keep the picture stable. Whether it's a video-cassette recorder or a camera, each video source contains its own pulse that synchronizes and generates the picture it's sending in order to keep it straight and steady. A video-cassette recorder must "lock up" to the sync pulses that are part of the video it's trying to record. If the device doesn't have gunlock, this effort must be very noticeable.
    B. A video signal or television is comprised of three parts: the black-and-white portion, the color portion, and the sync (synchronizing) pulses, which keep the picture stable. Whether it's a camera or a video-cassette recorder, each video source contains its own generator of these synchronizing pulses. These accompany the picture that it's sending in order to keep it straight and steady. A video-cassette recorder must "lock up" to the sync pulses that are part of the video it is trying to record in order to produce a clean recording. This effort may be very noticeable if the device does not have gunlock.
    C. There are three parts to a television or video signal: the color portion, the black-and-white portion, and the sync (synchronizing pulses). These keep the picture stable. Each video source, whether it's a video-cassette recorder or a camera, generates these synchronizing pulses accompanying the picture it's sending in order to keep it straight and steady. If a clean recording is to be produced, a video-cassette recorder must store the sync pulses that are part of the video it is trying to record. This effort may not be noticeable if the device does not have gunlock.
    D. A television signal or video signal has three parts: the black-and-white portion, the color portion, and the synchronizing (sync) pulses. It's the sync pulses which keep the picture stable, which accompany it and keep it steady and straight. Whether it's a camera or a video-cassette recorder, each video source contains its own generator of these synchronizing pulses. To produce a clean recording, a video-cassette recorder must "lock up" to the sync pulses that are part of the video it is trying to record. If the device does not have gunlock, this effort may be very noticeable.

10._____

KEY (CORRECT ANSWERS)

1.	C	6.	A
2.	B	7.	B
3.	A	8.	D
4.	B	9.	C
5.	D	10.	D

PHILOSOPHY, PRINCIPLES, PRACTICES, AND TECHNICS OF SUPERVISION, ADMINISTRATION, MANAGEMENT, AND ORGANIZATION

TABLE OF CONTENTS

	Page
MEANING OF SUPERVISION	1
THE OLD AND THE NEW SUPERVISION	1
THE EIGHT (8) BASIC PRINCIPLES OF THE NEW SUPERVISION	1
I. Principle of Responsibility	1
II. Principle of Authority	2
III. Principle of Self-Growth	2
IV. Principle of Individual Worth	2
V. Principle of Creative Leadership	2
VI. Principle of Success and Failure	2
VII. Principle of Science	3
VIII. Principle of Cooperation	3
WHAT IS ADMINISTRATION?	3
I. Practices Commonly Classed as "Supervisory"	3
II. Practices Commonly Classed as "Administrative"	3
III. Practices Commonly Classed as Both "Supervisory" and "Administrative"	4
RESPONSIBILITIES OF THE SUPERVISOR	4
COMPETENCIES OF THE SUPERVISOR	4
THE PROFESSIONAL SUPERVISOR-EMPLOYEE RELATIONSHIP	4
MINI-TEXT IN SUPERVISION, ADMINISTRATION, MANAGEMENT, AND ORGANIZATION	5
I. Brief Highlights	5
A. Levels of Management	6
B. What the Supervisor Must Learn	6
C. A Definition of Supervision	6
D. Elements of the Team Concept	6
E. Principles of Organization	6
F. The Four Important Parts of Every Job	7
G. Principles of Delegation	7
H. Principles of Effective Communications	7
I. Principles of Work Improvement	7
J. Areas of Job Improvement	7
K. Seven Key Points in Making Improvements	8

	L.	Corrective Techniques for Job Improvement	8
	M.	A Planning Checklist	8
	N.	Five Characteristics of Good Directions	9
	O.	Types of Directions	9
	P.	Controls	9
	Q.	Orienting the New Employee	9
	R.	Checklist for Orienting New Employees	9
	S.	Principles of Learning	10
	T.	Causes of Poor Performance	10
	U.	Four Major Steps in On-the-Job Instructions	10
	V.	Employees Want Five Things	10
	W.	Some Don'ts in Regard to Praise	11
	X.	How to Gain Your Workers' Confidence	11
	Y.	Sources of Employee Problems	11
	Z.	The Supervisor's Key to Discipline	11
	AA.	Five Important Processes of Management	12
	BB.	When the Supervisor Fails to Plan	12
	CC.	Fourteen General Principles of Management	12
	DD.	Change	12

II. Brief Topical Summaries — 13
　　A. Who/What is the Supervisor? — 13
　　B. The Sociology of Work — 13
　　C. Principles and Practices of Supervision — 14
　　D. Dynamic Leadership — 14
　　E. Processes for Solving Problems — 15
　　F. Training for Results — 15
　　G. Health, Safety, and Accident Prevention — 16
　　H. Equal Employment Opportunity — 16
　　I. Improving Communications — 16
　　J. Self-Development — 17
　　K. Teaching and Training — 17
　　　　1. The Teaching Process — 17
　　　　　　a. Preparation — 17
　　　　　　b. Presentation — 18
　　　　　　c. Summary — 18
　　　　　　d. Application — 18
　　　　　　e. Evaluation — 18
　　　　2. Teaching Methods — 18
　　　　　　a. Lecture — 18
　　　　　　b. Discussion — 18
　　　　　　c. Demonstration — 19
　　　　　　d. Performance — 19
　　　　　　e. Which Method to Use — 19

PHILOSOPHY, PRINCIPLES, PRACTICES, AND TECHNICS OF SUPERVISION, ADMINISTRATION, MANAGEMENT, AND ORGANIZATION

MEANING OF SUPERVISION

The extension of the democratic philosophy has been accompanied by an extension in the scope of supervision. Modern leaders and supervisors no longer think of supervision in the narrow sense of being confined chiefly to visiting employees, supplying materials, or rating the staff. They regard supervision as being intimately related to all the concerned agencies of society, they speak of the supervisor's function in terms of "growth," rather than the "improvement" of employees.

This modern concept of supervision may be defined as follows: Supervision is leadership and the development of leadership within groups which are cooperatively engaged in inspection, research, training, guidance, and evaluation.

THE OLD AND THE NEW SUPERVISION

TRADITIONAL
1. Inspection
2. Focused on the employee
3. Visitation
4. Random and haphazard
5. Imposed and authoritarian
6. One person usually

MODERN
1. Study and analysis
2. Focused on aims, materials, methods, supervisors, employees, environment
3. Demonstrations, intervisitation, workshops, directed reading, bulletins, etc.
4. Definitely organized and planned (scientific)
5. Cooperative and democratic
6. Many persons involved (creative)

THE EIGHT (8) BASIC PRINCIPLES OF THE NEW SUPERVISION

I. Principle of Responsibility
   Authority to act and responsibility for acting must be joined.
   A. If you give responsibility, give authority.
   B. Define employee duties clearly.
   C. Protect employees from criticism by others.
   D. Recognize the rights as well as obligations of employees.
   E. Achieve the aims of a democratic society insofar as it is possible within the area of your work.
   F. Establish a situation favorable to training and learning.
   G. Accept ultimate responsibility for everything done in your section, unit, office, division, department.
   H. Good administration and good supervision are inseparable.

II. Principle of Authority
The success of the supervisor is measured by the extent to which the power of authority is not used.
   A. Exercise simplicity and informality in supervision
   B. Use the simplest machinery of supervision
   C. If it is good for the organization as a whole, it is probably justified.
   D. Seldom be arbitrary or authoritative.
   E. Do not base your work on the power of position or of personality.
   F. Permit and encourage the free expression of opinions.

III. Principle of Self-Growth
The success of the supervisor is measured by the extent to which, and the speed with which, he is no longer needed.
   A. Base criticism on principles, not on specifics.
   B. Point out higher activities to employees.
   C. Train for self-thinking by employees to meet new situations.
   D. Stimulate initiative, self-reliance, and individual responsibility
   E. Concentrate on stimulating the growth of employees rather than on removing defects.

IV. Principle of Individual Worth
Respect for the individual is a paramount consideration in supervision.
   A. Be human and sympathetic in dealing with employees.
   B. Don't nag about things to be done.
   C. Recognize the individual differences among employees and seek opportunities to permit best expression of each personality.

V. Principle of Creative Leadership
The best supervision is that which is not apparent to the employee.
   A. Stimulate, don't drive employees to creative action.
   B. Emphasize doing good things.
   C. Encourage employees to do what they do best.
   D. Do not be too greatly concerned with details of subject or method.
   E. Do not be concerned exclusively with immediate problems and activities.
   F. Reveal higher activities and make them both desired and maximally possible.
   G. Determine procedures in the light of each situation but see that these are derived from a sound basic philosophy.
   H. Aid, inspire, and lead so as to liberate the creative spirit latent in all good employees.

VI. Principle of Success and Failure
There are no unsuccessful employees, only unsuccessful supervisors who have failed to give proper leadership.
   A. Adapt suggestions to the capacities, attitudes, and prejudices of employees.
   B. Be gradual, be progressive, be persistent.
   C. Help the employee find the general principle; have the employee apply his own problem to the general principle.
   D. Give adequate appreciation for good work and honest effort.
   E. Anticipate employee difficulties and help to prevent them.
   F. Encourage employees to do the desirable things they will do anyway.
   G. Judge your supervision by the results it secures.

VII. Principle of Science
Successful supervision is scientific, objective, and experimental. It is based on facts, not on prejudices.
   A. Be cumulative in results.
   B. Never divorce your suggestions from the goals of training.
   C. Don't be impatient of results.
   D. Keep all matters on a professional, not a personal, level.
   E. Do not be concerned exclusively with immediate problems and activities.
   F. Use objective means of determining achievement and rating where possible.

VIII. Principle of Cooperation
Supervision is a cooperative enterprise between supervisor and employee.
   A. Begin with conditions as they are.
   B. Ask opinions of all involved when formulating policies.
   C. Organization is as good as its weakest link.
   D. Let employees help to determine policies and department programs.
   E. Be approachable and accessible—physically and mentally.
   F. Develop pleasant social relationships.

WHAT IS ADMINISTRATION

Administration is concerned with providing the environment, the material facilities, and the operational procedures that will promote the maximum growth and development of supervisors and employees. (Organization is an aspect and a concomitant of administration.)

There is no sharp line of demarcation between supervision and administration; these functions are intimately interrelated and, often, overlapping. They are complementary activities.

I. Practices Commonly Classed as "Supervisory"
   A. Conducting employees' conferences
   B. Visiting sections, units, offices, divisions, departments
   C. Arranging for demonstrations
   D. Examining plans
   E. Suggesting professional reading
   F. Interpreting bulletins
   G. Recommending in-service training courses
   H. Encouraging experimentation
   I. Appraising employee morale
   J. Providing for intervisitation

II. Practices Commonly Classified as "Administrative"
   A. Management of the office
   B. Arrangement of schedules for extra duties
   C. Assignment of rooms or areas
   D. Distribution of supplies
   E. Keeping records and reports
   F. Care of audio-visual materials
   G. Keeping inventory records
   H. Checking record cards and books

    I.   Programming special activities
    J.   Checking on the attendance and punctuality of employees

III. Practices Commonly Classified as Both "Supervisory" and "Administrative"
    A. Program construction
    B. Testing or evaluating outcomes
    C. Personnel accounting
    D. Ordering instructional materials

RESPONSIBILITIES OF THE SUPERVISOR

A person employed in a supervisory capacity must constantly be able to improve his own efficiency and ability. He represent the employer to the employees and only continuous self-examination can make him a capable supervisor.

Leadership and training are the supervisor's responsibility. An efficient working unit is one in which the employees work with the supervisor. It is his job to bring out the best in his employees. He must always be relaxed, courteous, and calm in his association with his employees. Their feelings are important, and a harsh attitude does not develop the most efficient employees.

COMPETENCES OF THE SUPERVISOR

    I.   Complete knowledge of the duties and responsibilities of his position.
    II.   To be able to organize a job, plan ahead, and carry through.
    III. To have self-confidence and initiative.
    IV. To be able to handle the unexpected situation and make quick decisions.
    V.   To be able to properly train subordinates in the positions they are best suited for.
    VI. To be able to keep good human relations among his subordinates.
    VII. To be able to keep good human relations between his subordinates and himself and to earn their respect and trust.

THE PROFESSIONAL SUPERVISOR-EMPLOYEE RELATIONSHIP

There are two kinds of efficiency: one kind is only apparent and is produced in organizations through the exercise of mere discipline; this is but a simulation of the second, or true, efficiency which springs from spontaneous cooperation. If you are a manager, no matter how great or small your responsibility, it is your job, in the final analysis, to create and develop this involuntary cooperation among the people whom you supervise. For, no matter how powerful a combination of money, machines, and materials a company may have, this is a dead and sterile thing without a team of willing, thinking, and articulate people to guide it.

The following 21 points are presented as indicative of the exemplary basic relationship that should exist between supervisor and employee:

1. Each person wants to be liked and respected by his fellow employee and wants to be treated with consideration and respect by his superior.
2. The most competent employee will make an error. However, in a unit where good relations exist between the supervisor and his employees, tenseness and fear do not exist. Thus, errors are not hidden or covered up, and the efficiency of a unit is not impaired.

3. Subordinates resent rules, regulations, or orders that are unreasonable or unexplained.
4. Subordinates are quick to resent unfairness, harshness, injustices, and favoritism.
5. An employee will accept responsibility if he knows that he will be complimented for a job well done, and not too harshly chastised for failure; that his supervisor will check the cause of the failure, and, if it was the supervisor's fault, he will assume the blame therefore. If it was the employee's fault, his supervisor will explain the correct method or means of handling the responsibility.
6. An employee wants to receive credit for a suggestion he has made, that is used. If a suggestion cannot be used, the employee is entitled to an explanation. The supervisor should not say "no" and close the subject.
7. Fear and worry slow up a worker's ability. Poor working environment can impair his physical and mental health. A good supervisor avoids forceful methods, threats, and arguments to get a job done.
8. A forceful supervisor is able to train his employees individually and as a team, and is able to motivate them in the proper channels.
9. A mature supervisor is able to properly evaluate his subordinates and to keep them happy and satisfied.
10. A sensitive supervisor will never patronize his subordinates.
11. A worthy supervisor will respect his employees' confidences.
12. Definite and clear-cut responsibilities should be assigned to each executive.
13. Responsibility should always be coupled with corresponding authority.
14. No change should be made in the scope or responsibilities of a position without a definite understanding to that effect on the part of all persons concerned.
15. No executive or employee, occupying a single position in the organization, should be subject to definite orders from more than one source.
16. Orders should never be given to subordinates over the head of a responsible executive. Rather than do this, the officer in question should be supplanted.
17. Criticisms of subordinates should, whoever possible, be made privately, and in no case should a subordinate be criticized in the presence of executives or employees of equal or lower rank.
18. No dispute or difference between executives or employees as to authority or responsibilities should be considered too trivial for prompt and careful adjudication.
19. Promotions, wage changes, and disciplinary action should always be approved by the executive immediately superior to the one directly responsible.
20. No executive or employee should ever be required, or expected, to be at the same time an assistant to, and critic of, another.
21. Any executive whose work is subject to regular inspection should, wherever practicable, be given the assistance and facilities necessary to enable him to maintain an independent check of the quality of his work.

MINI-TEXT IN SUPERVISION, ADMINISTRATION, MANAGEMENT, AND ORGANIZATION

I. Brief Highlights

Listed concisely and sequentially are major headings and important data in the field for quick recall and review.

A. Levels of Management
    Any organization of some size has several levels of management. In terms of a ladder, the levels are:

    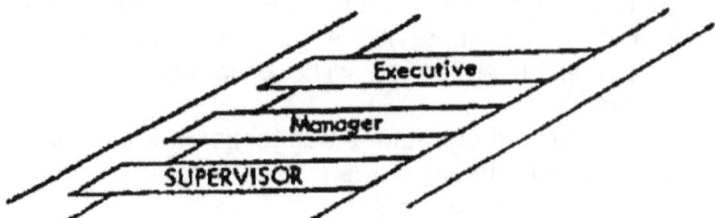

    The first level is very important because it is the beginning point of management leadership.

B. What the Supervisor Must Learn
    A supervisor must learn to:
    1. Deal with people and their differences
    2. Get the job done through people
    3. Recognize the problems when they exist
    4. Overcome obstacles to good performance
    5. Evaluate the performance of people
    6. Check his own performance in terms of accomplishment

C. A Definition of Supervisor
    The term supervisor means any individual having authority, in the interests of the employer, to hire, transfer, suspend, lay-off, recall, promote, discharge, assign, reward, or discipline other employees or responsibility to direct them, or to adjust their grievances, or effectively to recommend such action, if, in connection with the foregoing, exercise of such authority is not of a merely routine or clerical nature but requires the use of independent judgment.

D. Elements of the Team Concept
    What is involved in teamwork? The component parts are:
    1. Members
    2. A leader
    3. Goals
    4. Plans
    5. Cooperation
    6. Spirit

E. Principles of Organization
    1. A team member must know what his job is.
    2. Be sure that the nature and scope of a job are understood.
    3. Authority and responsibility should be carefully spelled out.
    4. A supervisor should be permitted to make the maximum number of decisions affecting his employees.
    5. Employees should report to only one supervisor.
    6. A supervisor should direct only as many employees as he can handle effectively.
    7. An organization plan should be flexible.

8. Inspection and performance of work should be separate.
9. Organizational problems should receive immediate attention.
10. Assign work in line with ability and experience.

F. The Four Important Parts of Every Job
1. Inherent in every job is the *accountability* for results.
2. A second set of factors in every job is *responsibilities*.
3. Along with duties and responsibilities one must have the *authority* to act within certain limits without obtaining permission to proceed.
4. No job exists in a vacuum. The supervisor is surrounded by key *relationships*.

G. Principles of Delegation
Where work is delegated for the first time, the supervisor should think in terms of these questions:
1. Who is best qualified to do this?
2. Can an employee improve his abilities by doing this?
3. How long should an employee spend on this?
4. Are there any special problems for which he will need guidance?
5. How broad a delegation can I make?

H. Principles of Effective Communications
1. Determine the media.
2. To whom directed?
3. Identification and source authority.
4. Is communication understood?

I. Principles of Work Improvement
1. Most people usually do only the work which is assigned to them.
2. Workers are likely to fit assigned work into the time available to perform it.
3. A good workload usually stimulates output.
4. People usually do their best work when they know that results will be reviewed or inspected.
5. Employees usually feel that someone else is responsible for conditions of work, workplace layout, job methods, type of tools/equipment, and other such factors.
6. Employees are usually defensive about their job security.
7. Employees have natural resistance to change.
8. Employees can support or destroy a supervisor.
9. A supervisor usually earns the respect of his people through his personal example of diligence and efficiency.

J. Areas of Job Improvement
The areas of job improvement are quite numerous, but the most common ones which a supervisor can identify and utilize are:
1. Departmental layout
2. Flow of work
3. Workplace layout
4. Utilization of manpower
5. Work methods
6. Materials handling

7. Utilization
8. Motion economy

K. Seven Key Points in Making Improvements
1. Select the job to be improved
2. Study how it is being done now
3. Question the present method
4. Determine actions to be taken
5. Chart proposed method
6. Get approval and apply
7. Solicit worker participation

L. Corrective Techniques of Job Improvement
Specific Problems
1. Size of workload
2. Inability to meet schedules
3. Strain and fatigue
4. Improper use of men and skills
5. Waste, poor quality, unsafe conditions
6. Bottleneck conditions that hinder output
7. Poor utilization of equipment and machine
8. Efficiency and productivity of labor

General Improvement
1. Departmental layout
2. Flow of work
3. Work plan layout
4. Utilization of manpower
5. Work methods
6. Materials handling
7. Utilization of equipment
8. Motion economy

Corrective Techniques
1. Study with scale model
2. Flow chart study
3. Motion analysis
4. Comparison of units produced to standard allowance
5. Methods analysis
6. Flow chart and equipment study
7. Down time vs. running time
8. Motion analysis

M. A Planning Checklist
1. Objectives
2. Controls
3. Delegations
4. Communications
5. Resources
6. Manpower

7. Equipment
8. Supplies and materials
9. Utilization of time
10. Safety
11. Money
12. Work
13. Timing of improvements

N. Five Characteristics of Good Directions
In order to get results, directions must be:
1. Possible of accomplishment
2. Agreeable with worker interests
3. Related to mission
4. Planned and complete
5. Unmistakably clear

O. Types of Directions
1. Demands or direct orders
2. Requests
3. Suggestion or implication
4. volunteering

P. Controls
A typical listing of the overall areas in which the supervisor should establish controls might be:
1. Manpower
2. Materials
3. Quality of work
4. Quantity of work
5. Time
6. Space
7. Money
8. Methods

Q. Orienting the New Employee
1. Prepare for him
2. Welcome the new employee
3. Orientation for the job
4. Follow-up

R. Checklist for Orienting New Employees   Yes   No
1. Do you appreciate the feelings of new employees
   when they first report for work?   ___   ___
2. Are you aware of the fact that the new employee must
   make a big adjustment to his job?   ___   ___
3. Have you given him good reasons for liking the job and
   the organization?   ___   ___
4. Have you prepared for his first day on the job?   ___   ___
5. Did you welcome him cordially and make him feel needed?   ___   ___

	Yes	No

6. Did you establish rapport with him so that he feels free to talk and discuss matters with you? ___ ___
7. Did you explain his job to him and his relationship to you? ___ ___
8. Does he know that his work will be evaluated periodically on a basis that is fair and objective? ___ ___
9. Did you introduce him to his fellow workers in such a way that they are likely to accept him? ___ ___
10. Does he know what employee benefits he will receive? ___ ___
11. Does he understand the importance of being on the job and what to do if he must leave his duty station? ___ ___
12. Has he been impressed with the importance of accident prevention and safe practice? ___ ___
13. Does he generally know his way around the department? ___ ___
14. Is he under the guidance of a sponsor who will teach the right way of doing things? ___ ___
15. Do you plan to follow-up so that he will continue to adjust successfully to his job? ___ ___

S. Principles of Learning
   1. Motivation
   2. Demonstration or explanation
   3. Practice

T. Causes of Poor Performance
   1. Improper training for job
   2. Wrong tools
   3. Inadequate directions
   4. Lack of supervisory follow-up
   5. Poor communications
   6. Lack of standards of performance
   7. Wrong work habits
   8. Low morale
   9. Other

U. Four Major Steps in On-The-Job Instruction
   1. Prepare the worker
   2. Present the operation
   3. Tryout performance
   4. Follow-up

V. Employees Want Five Things
   1. Security
   2. Opportunity
   3. Recognition
   4. Inclusion
   5. Expression

W. Some Don'ts in Regard to Praise
   1. Don't praise a person for something he hasn't done.
   2. Don't praise a person unless you can be sincere.
   3. Don't be sparing in praise just because your superior withholds it from you.
   4. Don't let too much time elapse between good performance and recognition of it

X. How to Gain Your Workers' Confidence
   Methods of developing confidence include such things as:
   1. Knowing the interests, habits, hobbies of employees
   2. Admitting your own inadequacies
   3. Sharing and telling of confidence in others
   4. Supporting people when they are in trouble
   5. Delegating matters that can be well handled
   6. Being frank and straightforward about problems and working conditions
   7. Encouraging others to bring their problems to you
   8. Taking action on problems which impede worker progress

Y. Sources of Employee Problems
   On-the-job causes might be such things as:
   1. A feeling that favoritism is exercised in assignments
   2. Assignment of overtime
   3. An undue amount of supervision
   4. Changing methods or systems
   5. Stealing of ideas or trade secrets
   6. Lack of interest in job
   7. Threat of reduction in force
   8. Ignorance or lack of communications
   9. Poor equipment
   10. Lack of knowing how supervisor feels toward employee
   11. Shift assignments

   Off-the-job problems might have to do with:
   1. Health
   2. Finances
   3. Housing
   4. Family

Z. The Supervisor's Key to Discipline
   There are several key points about discipline which the supervisor should keep in mind:
   1. Job discipline is one of the disciplines of life and is directed by the supervisor.
   2. It is more important to correct an employee fault than to fix blame for it.
   3. Employee performance is affected by problems both on the job and off.
   4. Sudden or abrupt changes in behavior can be indications of important employee problems.
   5. Problems should be dealt with as soon as possible after they are identified.
   6. The attitude of the supervisor may have more to do with solving problems than the techniques of problem solving.
   7. Correction of employee behavior should be resorted to only after the supervisor is sure that training or counseling will not be helpful.

8. Be sure to document your disciplinary actions.
9. Make sure that you are disciplining on the basis of facts rather than personal feelings.
10. Take each disciplinary step in order, being careful not to make snap judgments, or decisions based on impatience.

AA. Five Important Processes of Management
1. Planning
2. Organizing
3. Scheduling
4. Controlling
5. Motivating

BB. When the Supervisor Fails to Plan
1. Supervisor creates impression of not knowing his job
2. May lead to excessive overtime
3. Job runs itself—supervisor lacks control
4. Deadlines and appointments missed
5. Parts of the work go undone
6. Work interrupted by emergencies
7. Sets a bad example
8. Uneven workload creates peaks and valleys
9. Too much time on minor details at expense of more important tasks

CC. Fourteen General Principles of Management
1. Division of work
2. Authority and responsibility
3. Discipline
4. Unity of command
5. Unity of direction
6. Subordination of individual interest to general interest
7. Remuneration of personnel
8. Centralization
9. Scalar chain
10. Order
11. Equity
12. Stability of tenure of personnel
13. Initiative
14. Esprit de corps

DD. Change

Bringing about change is perhaps attempted more often, and yet less well understood, than anything else the supervisor does. How do people generally react to change? (People tend to resist change that is imposed upon them by other individuals or circumstances.

Change is characteristic of every situation. It is a part of every real endeavor where the efforts of people are concerned.

1. Why do people resist change?
   People may resist change because of:
   a. Fear of the unknown
   b. Implied criticism
   c. Unpleasant experiences in the past
   d. Fear of loss of status
   e. Threat to the ego
   f. Fear of loss of economic stability

2. How can we best overcome the resistance to change?
   In initiating change, take these steps:
   a. Get ready to sell
   b. Identify sources of help
   c. Anticipate objections
   d. Sell benefits
   e. Listen in depth
   f. Follow up

II. Brief Topical Summaries

   A. Who/What is the Supervisor?
      1. The supervisor is often called the "highest level employee and the lowest level manager."
      2. A supervisor is a member of both management and the work group. He acts as a bridge between the two.
      3. Most problems in supervision are in the area of human relations, or people problems.
      4. Employees expect: Respect, opportunity to learn and to advance, and a sense of belonging, and so forth.
      5. Supervisors are responsible for directing people and organizing work. Planning is of paramount importance.
      6. A position description is a set of duties and responsibilities inherent to a given position.
      7. It is important to keep the position description up-to-date and to provide each employee with his own copy.

   B. The Sociology of Work
      1. People are alike in many ways; however, each individual is unique.
      2. The supervisor is challenged in getting to know employee differences. Acquiring skills in evaluating individuals is an asset.
      3. Maintaining meaningful working relationships in the organization is of great importance.
      4. The supervisor has an obligation to help individuals to develop to their fullest potential.
      5. Job rotation on a planned basis helps to build versatility and to maintain interest and enthusiasm in work groups.
      6. Cross training (job rotation) provides backup skills.

14

7. The supervisor can help reduce tension by maintaining a sense of humor, providing guidance to employees, and by making reasonable and timely decisions. Employees respond favorably to working under reasonably predictable circumstances.
8. Change is characteristic of all managerial behavior. The supervisor must adjust to changes in procedures, new methods, technological changes, and to a number of new and sometimes challenging situations.
9. To overcome the natural tendency for people to resist change, the supervisor should become more skillful in initiating change.

C. Principles and Practices of Supervision
1. Employees should be required to answer to only one superior.
2. A supervisor can effectively direct only a limited number of employees, depending upon the complexity, variety, and proximity of the jobs involved.
3. The organizational chart presents the organization in graphic form. It reflects lines of authority and responsibility as well as interrelationships of units within the organization.
4. Distribution of work can be improved through an analysis using the "Work Distribution Chart."
5. The "Work Distribution Chart" reflects the division of work within a unit in understandable form.
6. When related tasks are given to an employee, he has a better chance of increasing his skills through training.
7. The individual who is given the responsibility for tasks must also be given the appropriate authority to insure adequate results.
8. The supervisor should delegate repetitive, routine work. Preparation of recurring reports, maintaining leave and attendance records are some examples.
9. Good discipline is essential to good task performance. Discipline is reflected in the actions of employees on the job in the absence of supervision.
10. Disciplinary action may have to be taken when the positive aspects of discipline have failed. Reprimand, warning, and suspension are examples of disciplinary action.
11. If a situation calls for a reprimand, be sure it is deserved and remember it is to be done in private.

D. Dynamic Leadership
1. A style is a personal method or manner of exerting influence.
2. Authoritarian leaders often see themselves as the source of power and authority.
3. The democratic leader often perceives the group as the source of authority and power.
4. Supervisors tend to do better when using the pattern of leadership that is most natural for them.
5. Social scientists suggest that the effective supervisor use the leadership style that best fits the problem or circumstances involved.
6. All four styles—telling, selling, consulting, joining—have their place. Using one does not preclude using the other at another time.

7. The theory X point of view assumes that the average person dislikes work, will avoid it whenever possible, and must be coerced to achieve organizational objectives.
8. The theory Y point of view assumes that the average person considers work to be a natural as play, and, when the individual is committed, he requires little supervision or direction to accomplish desired objectives.
9. The leader's basic assumptions concerning human behavior and human nature affect his actions, decisions, and other managerial practices.
10. Dissatisfaction among employees is often present, but difficult to isolate. The supervisor should seek to weaken dissatisfaction by keeping promises, being sincere and considerate, keeping employees informed, and so forth.
11. Constructive suggestions should be encouraged during the natural progress of the work.

E. Processes for Solving Problems
1. People find their daily tasks more meaningful and satisfying when they can improve them.
2. The causes of problems, or the key factors, are often hidden in the background. Ability to solve problems often involves the ability to isolate them from their backgrounds. There is some substance to the cliché that some persons "can't see the forest for the trees."
3. New procedures are often developed from old ones. Problems should be broken down into manageable parts. New ideas can be adapted from old one.
4. People think differently in problem-solving situations. Using a logical, patterned approach is often useful. One approach found to be useful includes these steps:
   a. Define the problem
   b. Establish objectives
   c. Get the facts
   d. Weigh and decide
   e. Take action
   f. Evaluate action

F. Training for Results
1. Participants respond best when they feel training is important to them.
2. The supervisor has responsibility for the training and development of those who report to him.
3. When training is delegated to others, great care must be exercised to insure the trainer has knowledge, aptitude, and interest for his work as a trainer.
4. Training (learning) of some type goes on continually. The most successful supervisor makes certain the learning contributes in a productive manner to operational goals.
5. New employees are particularly susceptible to training. Older employees facing new job situations require specific training, as well as having need for development and growth opportunities.
6. Training needs require continuous monitoring.
7. The training officer of an agency is a professional with a responsibility to assist supervisors in solving training problems.

16

8. Many of the self-development steps important to the supervisor's own growth are equally important to the development of peers and subordinates. Knowledge of these is important when the supervisor consults with others on development and growth opportunities.

G. Health, Safety, and Accident Prevention
1. Management-minded supervisors take appropriate measures to assist employees in maintaining health and in assuring safe practices in the work environment.
2. Effective safety training and practices help to avoid injury and accidents.
3. Safety should be a management goal. All infractions of safety which are observed should be corrected without exception.
4. Employees' safety attitude, training and instruction, provision of safe tools and equipment, supervision, and leadership are considered highly important factors which contribute to safety and which can be influenced directly by supervisors.
5. When accidents do occur, they should be investigated promptly for very important reasons, including the fact that information which is gained can be used to prevent accidents in the future.

H. Equal Employment Opportunity
1. The supervisor should endeavor to treat all employees fairly, without regard to religion, race, sex, or national origin.
2. Groups tend to reflect the attitude of the leader. Prejudice can be detected even in very subtle form. Supervisors must strive to create a feeling of mutual respect and confidence in every employee.
3. Complete utilization of all human resources is a national goal. Equitable consideration should be accorded women in the work force, minority-group members, the physically and mentally handicapped, and the older employee. The important question is: "Who can do the job?"
4. Training opportunities, recognition for performance, overtime assignments, promotional opportunities, and all other personnel actions are to be handled on an equitable basis.

I. Improving Communications
1. Communications is achieving understanding between the sender and the receiver of a message. It also means sharing information—the creation of understanding.
2. Communication is basic to all human activity. Words are means of conveying meanings; however, real meanings are in people.
3. There are very practical differences in the effectiveness of one-way, impersonal, and two-way communications. Words spoken face-to-face are better understood. Telephone conversations are effective, but lack the rapport of person-to-person exchanges. The whole person communicates.
4. Cooperation and communication in an organization go hand in hand. When there is a mutual respect between people, spelling out rules and procedures for communicating is unnecessary.
5. There are several barriers to effective communications. These include failure to listen with respect and understanding, lack of skill in feedback, and misinterpreting the meanings of words used by the speaker. It is also common

practice to listen to what we want to hear, and tune out things we do not want to hear.
6. Communication is management's chief problem. The supervisor should accept the challenge to communicate more effectively and to improve interagency and intra-agency communications.
7. The supervisor may often plan for and conduct meetings. The planning phase is critical and may determine the success or the failure of a meeting.
8. Speaking before groups usually requires extra effort. Stage fright may never disappear completely, but it can be controlled.

J. Self-Development
1. Every employee is responsible for his own self-development.
2. Toastmaster and toastmistress clubs offer opportunities to improve skills in oral communications.
3. Planning for one's own self-development is of vital importance. Supervisors know their own strengths and limitations better than anyone else.
4. Many opportunities are open to aid the supervisor in his developmental efforts, including job assignments; training opportunities, both governmental and non-governmental—to include universities and professional conferences and seminars.
5. Programmed instruction offers a means of studying at one's own rate.
6. Where difficulties may arise from a supervisor's being away from his work for training, he may participate in televised home study or correspondence courses to meet his self-development needs.

K. Teaching and Training
1. The Teaching Process
Teaching is encouraging and guiding the learning activities of students toward established goals. In most cases this process consists of five steps: preparation, presentation, summarization, evaluation, and application.

   a. Preparation
   Preparation is two-fold in nature; that of the supervisor and the employee. Preparation by the supervisor is absolutely essential to success. He must know what, when, where, how, and whom he will teach. Some of the factors that should be considered are:
   1) The objectives
   2) The materials needed
   3) The methods to be used
   4) Employee participation
   5) Employee interest
   6) Training aids
   7) Evaluation
   8) Summarization

   Employee preparation consists in preparing the employee to receive the material. Probably the most important single factor in the preparation of the employee is arousing and maintaining his interest. He must know the objectives of the training, why he is there, how the material can be used, and its importance to him.

b. Presentation
In presentation, have a carefully designed plan and follow it. The plan should be accurate and complete, yet flexible enough to meet situations as they arise. The method of presentation will be determined by the particular situation and objectives.

c. Summary
A summary should be made at the end of every training unit and program. In addition, there may be internal summaries depending on the nature of the material being taught. The important thing is that the trainee must always be able to understand how each part of the new material relates to the whole.

d. Application
The supervisor must arrange work so the employee will be given a chance to apply new knowledge or skills while the material is still clear in his mind and interest is high. The trainee does not really know whether he has learned the material until he has been given a chance to apply it. If the material is not applied, it loses most of its value.

e. Evaluation
The purpose of all training is to promote learning. To determine whether the training has been a success or failure, the supervisor must evaluate this learning.
In the broadest sense, evaluation includes all the devices, methods, skills, and techniques used by the supervisor to keep himself and the employees informed as to their progress toward the objectives they are pursuing. The extent to which the employee has mastered the knowledge, skills, and abilities, or changed his attitudes, as determined by the program objectives, is the extent to which instruction has succeeded or failed.
Evaluation should not be confined to the end of the lesson, day, or program but should be used continuously. We shall note later the way this relates to the rest of the teaching process.

2. Teaching Methods
A teaching method is a pattern of identifiable student and instructor activity used in presenting training material.
All supervisors are faced with the problem of deciding which method should be used at a given time.

a. Lecture
The lecture is direct oral presentation of material by the supervisor. The present trend is to place less emphasis on the trainer's activity and more on that of the trainee.

b. Discussion
Teaching by discussion or conference involves using questions and other techniques to arouse interest and focus attention upon certain areas, and by doing so creating a learning situation. This can be one of the most

valuable methods because it gives the employees an opportunity to express their ideas and pool their knowledge.

    c. Demonstration
The demonstration is used to teach how something works or how to do something. It can be used to show a principle or what the results of a series of actions will be. A well-staged demonstration is particularly effective because it shows proper methods of performance in a realistic manner.

    d. Performance
Performance is one of the most fundamental of all learning techniques or teaching methods. The trainee may be able to tell how a specific operation should be performed but he cannot be sure he knows how to perform the operation until he has done so.
As with all methods, there are certain advantages and disadvantages to each method.

    e. Which Method to Use
Moreover, there are other methods and techniques of teaching. It is difficult to use any method without other methods entering into it. In any learning situation, a combination of methods is usually more effective than any one method alone.

Finally, evaluation must be integrated into the other aspects of the teaching-learning process.

It must be used in the motivation of the trainees; it must be used to assist in developing understanding during the training; and it must be related to employee application of the results of training.

This is distinctly the role of the supervisor.

GLOSSARY OF SHIPPING TERMS AND ABBREVIATIONS

A

a.a.x - Against all risks
ADDRESS - A particular street address (not a U.S. Post Office Box Number), which must include the Post Office Zip Code.
a.d. - After date.
AD. VAL. - According to value (Ad Valorem).
AD VALOREM - A freight rate set at a certain percentage of the value of an article is known as an ad valorem rate.
ANY QUANTITY - Rates are applicable regardless of quantity or weight.
A.1 - First class condition.
AQ - Any quantity.
AVDP. - Avoirdupois.

B

B&SG - Browne & Sharpe gauge
bbl. - Barrel.
B.D.I. - Both dates inclusive
B/E - Bill of exchange.
B/L - Bill of lading.
B.O. - Bad order; Buyer's option.
B/P - Bills payable.
bu. - Bushel.
BULK CARRIER - A bulk carrier is a vessel engaged in the carriage of such bulk commodities as petroleum, grain, or ores which are not packaged, bundled, bottled, or otherwise packed.
BWG - Birmingham wire gauge
bx. - Box.

C

C&F - Cost and freight; the same as c.i.f., except that insurance
is arranged by the buyer.
c.c. - Current cost.
c.f. - Cubic foot.
c.i. - Cost and insurance.
c/i - Certificate of insurance.
CIF - Cost, insurance, and freight: a price quotation under which the exporter quotes a price that includes prepayment of freight charges and insurance to an agreed destination
c.i.f.& e. - Cost, insurance, freight & exchange.
C.O.D. - Cash on delivery; Collection on delivery.
C.O.S. - Cash on shipment.
C.R. – Carrier's risk.
c.t.l.o. - Constructive total loss only. cu. ft. - Cubic feet.
cwt. - Hundredweight.

D

D.A. - Documents for acceptance.
D/A - Days after acceptance.
DAT - Dangerous articles tariff.
d/b/a - Doing business as.
D.D. - Demand draft.
D/D - Date draft
d.d.e. - Dispatch discharging only.

DEFERRED REBATE - A deferred rebate is the return of a portion of the freight charges by a carrier or a conference to a shipper in exchange for the shipper giving all or most of his shipments to the carrier or conference over a specified period of time (usually six months). Payment of the rebate is deferred for a further similar period, during which the shipper must continue to give all or most of his shipments to the rebating carrier or conference. The shipper thus earns a further rebate which will not, however, be paid without an additional period of exclusive or almost exclusive patronage with the carrier or conference. In this way, the shipper becomes tied to the rebating carrier or conference. Although the deferred rebate system is illegal in U.S. foreign commerce, it generally is accepted in the ocean trade between foreign countries.

DENSITY - Density means pounds per cubic foot.

The cubage of loose articles or pieces, or packaged articles of a rectangular, elliptical or square shape on one plane shall be determined by multiplying the greatest straight line dimensions of length, width and depth in inches, including all projections, and dividing the total by 1728 (to obtain cubic feet). The density is the weight of the article divided by the cubic feet thus obtained.

d.l.o. - Dispatch loading only.
dm. - Decimeter.
DM. - Dekameter.
DOT - Department of Transportation.
D.P. - Documents for payment.
d.p. - Direct port.
D/S - Days after sight.
d.w. - Deadweight (tons of 2240 lbs.).
d.w.c. - Deadweight for cargo.

E

E.A.O.N. - Expect as otherwise noted.
E.&.O.E. - Errors and omissions excepted.
E.E. - Errors excepted.
e.g. - For example.
est. - Estimated
est. wt. - Estimated weight.
et.al. - And others

F

f.a.c. - Fast as you can.
FAS - Free along side (vessel): a price quotation under which the exporter quotes a price that includes delivery of the goods to the vessel's side and within reach of its loading tackle. Subsequent risks and expenses are for the account of the buyer.
f.d. - Free discharge.
f.i.o. - Free in and out.
f.i.w. - Free in wagon.
FINISHED - Wooden articles that have passed the state of manufacture "in the white."
    (See IN THE WHITE)
F.M. - Fine measurement.
fms. - Fathoms.
FOB - Free on board (vessel) a price quotation under which the exporter quotes a price that includes delivery of the goods on board the vessel. Subsequent risks and expenses are for the account of the buyer. The term FOB may also be used in conjunction with an inland shipping point in the country of exportation or an inland point in the country of destination. This means that the expenses up to the point specified are for the account of the seller.

FOLDED - An article folded in such a manner as to reduce its bulk 33 1/3% from its normal shipping cubage when not folded.

FOLDED FLAT - An article folded in such a manner as to reduce its bulk 66 2/3% from its normal shipping cubage when not folded.

f.o.r. - Free on rail.

f.r.&c.c. - Free on riot & civil commotion.

ft. - Foot.

G

GAUGE - Where tariffs refer to gauge, they mean the U.S. standard Gauge for determining thickness of sheet or plate steel: Browne & Sharpe Gauge for rods and sheets of aluminum copper, brass and bronze; U. S. Steel Wire Gauge for iron and steel wire.

gm. - Gram.

G.T. - Gross ton.

H

hf. - Half.

hhd. - Hogshead.

ht. - Height.

I

ICC - Interstate Commerce Commission.

IN THE ROUGH - Wooden articles that are not further manufactured than sawn, hewn, planed, bent or turned.

IN THE WHITE - Wooden articles that are further manufactured than "in the rough," but including not more than one coat of priming.

inv. - Invoice

K

KD - Knocked down.

kg. - Kilogram.

KD FLAT - An article taken apart, folded or telescoped to reduce its bulk at least 66 2/3% below its assembled size.

KNOCKED DOWN (KD) - An article taken apart folded or telescoped in such a manner as to reduce its bulk at least 33 1/3% below its assembled bulk.

L

L.&D. - Loss and damage.

L.A. - Letter of authority.

L/C - Letter of credit.

L.C.L. - Less than carload.

l.c.m. - Least common multiple.

ldg. - Loading

LESS THAN TRUCKLOAD (LTL) - Rates applicable when the quantity of freight is less than the volume or truckload minimum weight.

LINER - A liner is a vessel, usually a common carrier, engaged in the carriage of general cargo along a definite route on a fixed schedule.

ltge. - Lighterage.

LTL - Less than truckload.

M

M.A. FORM - Special form of invoice required for shipment to Canada.
MDSE. - Merchandise.
MEASUREMENT TON - The measurement ton (also known as the cargo ton or freight ton) is a space measurement, usually 40 cubic feet or one cubic meter. The cargo is assessed a certain rate for every 40 cubic feet of space it occupies.
min. wt. - Minimum weight.
MW - Minimum weight factor.

N

NESTED - Three or more different sizes of an article are placed within each other so that each article will not project above the next lower article by more than 33 1/3% of its height.
NESTED SOLID - Three or more different sizes of an article are placed within each other so that each article will not project above the next lower article by more than 1/4 inch.
NMFC - National Motor Freight Classification.
N.O.E. - Not otherwise enumerated.
N.O.H.P. - Not otherwise herein provided.
N.O.I. - Not more specifically described.
N.O.I.B.N. - Not otherwise indicated by number; Not otherwise indicated by name.
N.O.S. - Not otherwise specified.
N.S.P.F. - Not specifically provided for.

O

O/A - Open account.
O/N - Order notify.
O.R. - Owners Risk.
O.S.&D. - Over, short and damage.
o.t. – On truck or railway

P

P.A. - Particular average.
P.D. - Per diem.
PLACE - A particular street address or other designation of a factory, store, warehouse, place of business, private residence, construction camp or the like, at a point (See POINT).
POINT - A particular city, town, village or other community or area which is treated as a unit for the application of rates.
PPD. - Prepaid.
PRO NUMBER - A number assigned by the carrier to a single shipment, used in all cases where the shipment must be referred to. Usually assigned at once.
P.W. - Packed weight.

R

REFG. - Refrigerating; Refrigeration.
R.I.T. - Refining in transit.
R.S. or L. - Classes the same or lower.

S

S.C. &S. - Strapped, corded and sealed.
S/D - Sight draft.
S.D.D. - Store door delivery.
sdg. - Siding
SET UP - Articles in their assembled condition.
SHIPMENT - A lot of freight tendered to a carrier by one consignor at one place at one time for delivery to one consignee at one place or one bill of lading.
S.I.T. - Stopping in transit.
SITE - A particular platform or location for loading or unloading at a place (See PLACE).
sld. - Sailed.
S.I. &C. - Shipper's load and count.
S.O. - Ship's option; Shipping order; seller's option.
S.S. - Shipside.
S/S - Steamship.
STDS. - Standards.
str. - Steamer.
S.U. - Set up.
S.U.C.l. - Set up carload.
S.U.I.C.L. - Set up in less than carload.

T

t/d/b/a - Trading and doing business as.
TL - Truckload.
t.l.o. - Total loss only.
TON - Freight rates for liner cargo generally are quoted on the basis of a certain rate per ton, depending on the nature of the commodity. This ton, however, may be a weight ton or a measurement ton.
TRAMP - A tramp ship is a vessel that does not operate along a definite route on a fixed schedule, but calls at any port where cargo is available.
TRUCKLOAD - Truckload rates apply where the tariff shows a truckload minimum weight. Charges will be at the truckload minimum weight unless weight is higher.

U

U.S.S.G. - U.S. standard guage.
u/w - Underwriter.

V

val. - Value.
VES. - Vessel.
viz. - Namely.
VOL. - Volume
VOLUME - Volume rates or classes are those for which a volume minimum weight (Vol. min. wt.) is provided; charges will be assessed at the volume minimum weight shown in the tariff except that actual weight will apply when in excess of the volume minimum weight.

W

W.&l. - Weighing and inspection.
W/B - Waybill.
w.p.a. - With particular average.

www.ingramcontent.com/pod-product-compliance
Lightning Source LLC
Chambersburg PA
CBHW082041300426
44117CB00015B/2564